YOU THINK IT STRANGE

'Ducks and geese rose quacking and honking out of the bay's salt marshes at daybreak as the charter boats headed for the Inlet. Ribbons of them streaked the skies heading north in spring and south in fall. Clouds of gulls wheeled above the bars and beyond the breakers off the beaches and dived on fleeing bait-fish. The sun rose like a new penny from the sea's edge as we'd head offshore; helmsmen squinted into it to avoid flotsam and keep their course. It died rose red and blinded them again when they were heading home. White caps form when the wind rises above ten knots and the sea backs glow mint-green. Beyond the 60-fathom line, ocean turns magnolia green. At sea there were no vomiting drunks, no aprons with rust-brown, dried pork blood, no customers demanding cuts from the front of the case, no cops on the take, no rats behind rice-sacks, no registers, no pushcart men and boys huddled round oil drum trash-fires waiting for trade. There were no Jews remembering pogroms, no hit men, no bullies. Barnegat Light was his Blessed Isles, and Joe fell in love with the sea.'

Dan Burt is a writer whose poetry and prose have appeared in *PN Review*, the *TLS*, the *Financial Times* and the *New Statesman*, among others. His writing draws on work as a butcher, mate, lawyer, public figure and businessman in, among other places, South Philadelphia; the sea off New Jersey; Washington, DC; New York; Boston; Riyadh, Saudi Arabia; and London. He lives and writes in London, Maine, and St John's College, Cambridge, of which he is an Honorary Fellow. www.danburtpoetry.com

Dan Burt

—

YOU THINK IT STRANGE

THE OVERLOOK PRESS
NEW YORK, NY

This edition first published in hardcover in the United States in 2015 by
The Overlook Press, Peter Mayer Publishers, Inc.

141 Wooster Street
New York, NY 10012
www.overlookpress.com

For bulk and special sales, please contact sales@overlookny.com,
or write us at the above address.

Library of Congress Cataloging-in-Publication Data
Burt, Dan M., 1942-
You think it strange : a memoir / Dan Burt.
pages cm
ISBN 978-1-4683-1125-9 (hardback)
1. Burt, Dan M., 1942---Childhood and youth. 2. Burt, Dan M., 1942---Family. 3. Poets, English--21st century--Biography. 4. South Philadelphia (Philadelphia, Pa.)--Biography. 5. Philadelphia (Pa.)--Biography. 6. Street life--Pennsylvania--Philadelphia--History--20th century. 7. Philadelphia (Pa.)--Social life and customs--20th century. 8. Philadelphia (Pa.)--Social conditions--20th century. 9. Americans--England--London--Biography. 10. Home--Psychological aspects. I. Title.
PR6102.U778Z46 2015
821'.92--dc23
[B]
2015011876

Manufactured in the United States of America
ISBN 978-1-4683-1125-9
2 4 6 8 10 9 7 5 3 1

For the Masters and Fellows
of St John's College, Cambridge

The Spur

You think it horrible that lust and rage
Should dance attention upon my old age;
They were not such a plague when I was young;
What else have I to spur me into song?

– W. B. Yeats, *New Poems* (1938)

from "In Memory of W. B. Yeats"

Time that with this strange excuse
Pardoned Kipling and his views,
And will pardon Paul Claudel,
Pardons him for writing well.

– W. H. Auden (pre-1966 version)

Contents

– I Certain Windows –

– II No Expectations –

– III The Blue Guitars –

– IV Envoi –

– Family Trees –

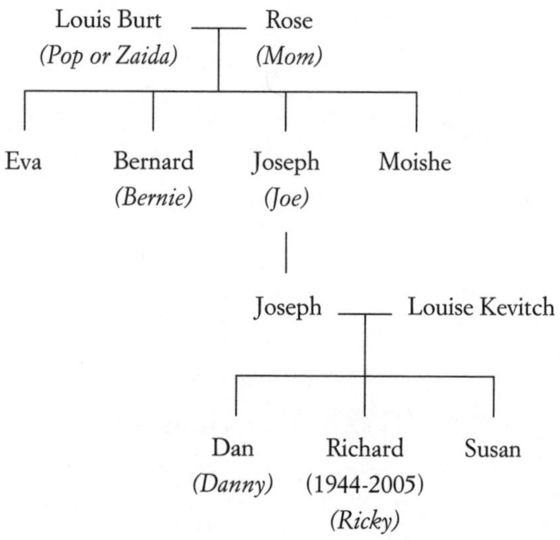

KEVITCH

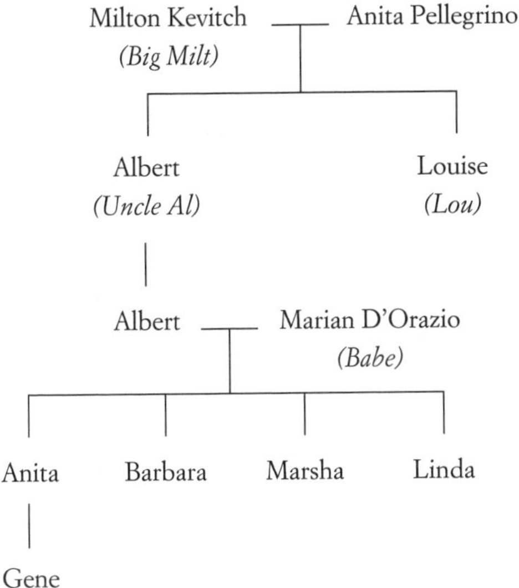

Milton Kevitch
(Big Milt)
Anita Pellegrino
Albert
(Uncle Al)
Louise
(Lou)
Albert
Marian D'Orazio
(Babe)
Anita
Barbara
Marsha
Linda
Gene

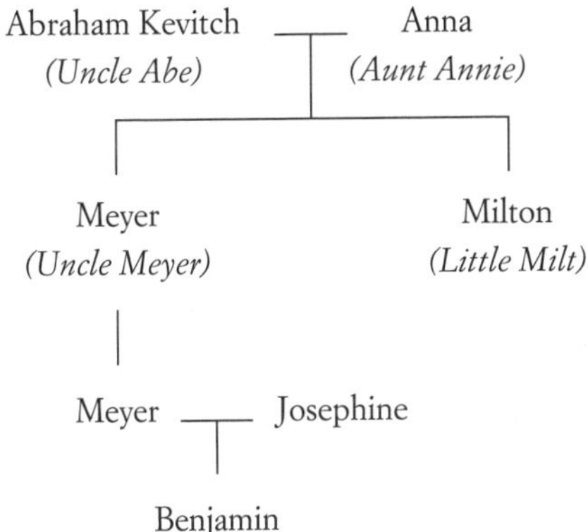

Abraham Kevitch
(Uncle Abe)
Anna
(Aunt Annie)
Meyer
(Uncle Meyer)
Milton
(Little Milt)
Meyer
Josephine
Benjamin

Author on 4th Street, 1945

At twelve I took a first step outside my ancestral world in Philadelphia's poorer neighborhoods. Ten years later I left their streets for Cambridge, England, and three decades later quit America for good. This is my recollection of the childhood and youth that made me an émigré.

I

– Certain Windows –

We trail no clouds of glory when we come. We trail blood, a cord that must be cut and a post-partum mess that mix with places, people, and stories to frame the house of childhood. We dwell in that house forever.

In time there will be others, bigger, smaller, better, worse; but how we see the world, how much shelter, warmth, food we think we need, whether the outer dark appears benign or deadly, depend on what we saw from certain windows in that house. We may burn, rebuild, repaint or raze it, but its memories fade least; as dementia settles in, first things are the last to go.

Childhood ended when I turned twelve and began working in a butcher shop on Fridays after school till midnight, and all day Saturdays from seven a.m. to six p.m., or, as we said in winter, "from can't see to can't see". By sixteen, I was working thirty hours a week or more during the school year, fifty to sixty hours in the summers. *Certain Windows* recalls my pre-travail world: places, people and tales from childhood.

ANCESTRAL HOUSES

Fourth and Daly

Joe Burt, my father, was born in Boston in 1916, almost nine months to the day after his mother landed there from a *shtetl* near Kiev. She brought with her Eva, her first born, and Bernie, her second. Presumably my grandfather, Louis (*Zaida* ["ai" as in "pay"] or Pop), was pleased to see my grandmother Rose, or Mom, even though she was generally regarded as a *chaleria*.[1]

Zaida had been dragooned into the Russian army a little before the outbreak of World War One. Russia levied a quota of Jewish men for the army from each *shtetl* and these men invariably came from the poorest *shtetlachim*.[2] *Zaida* deserted at the earliest opportunity, which was certainly not unusual, made his way to Boston and sent for Mom.

Mom and Pop moved the family in 1917 to a small row house at Fourth and Daly in South Philadelphia, the city where my father grew up, worked, married and in 1995 died. Pop was a carpenter, Mom a seamstress, both socialists at least, if not Communists. Mom was an organiser for the ILGWU,[3] which seems in character. Yiddish was

1. Yiddish for shrew.

2. Shetl dwellers.

3. International Ladies' Garment Workers Union.

the household tongue, my father's first, though Pop spoke and read Russian and English fluently. Mom managed Russian well, but English took more effort.

The family's daily newspaper was *Forverts*,[4] printed in Yiddish. *Forverts* published lists of those killed in pogroms when they occurred. Ukranian Cossacks allied themselves with the Bolsheviks and used the Russian civil war as an excuse to continue the pogroms that had been a fact of Jewish life in the Pale from the 1880s. Pop was hanging from a trolley car-strap on his way home from work in 1920 when he read the names of his family among the dead, all eighteen of them: father, mother, sisters, brothers, their children. He had become an orphan. He never went to *schul*[5] again.

A few years later he learned how they were killed, when some of Mom's family, who had hidden during the raid, emigrated to America. I heard the story from him when I was ten, at Christmas 1952. I came home singing "Silent Night", newly learned in my local public elementary school. I couldn't stop singing it and went carolling up the back steps from the alley into our kitchen where Pop, putty-coloured, in his mid-sixties and dying of cancer, was making what turned out to be his last visit. *Zaida* had cause to dislike Gentile sacred songs, though I didn't know it. He

4. *The Forward.*
5. Synagogue.

croaked, "Danila, shah stil",[6] and I answered, "No, why should I?" His face flushed with all the life left in him and he grabbed me by the neck and started choking. My father pulled him off, pinioned his arms, and, when his rage had passed, led me to the kitchen table where *Zaida* sat at the head and told me this story:

The Jews had warning of a raid. Pop's father, my great-grandfather, was pious and reputed to be a *melamed*, a learned though poor orthodox Jew. As such he was prized and protected by the community. Pop's in-laws urged him to take his family and hide with them in their shelter below the street. Great-grandfather refused. He said, so I was told, "God will protect us".

The Cossacks rousted them from their house and forced everyone to strip. They raped the women while the men watched. Done, they shot the women, then the children and, last, the men. They murdered all eighteen of them, my every paternal forebear excepting Pop, who died an atheist, as did my father.

My grandparents' house at Fourth and Daly was a three-up, three-down row (terraced) home on a very narrow street. Cars parked on the side of the street opposite their house, leaving just enough room for a small car to pass. Big-finned 1950s Caddies,

6. 'Danny, shut up.'

had anyone owned one, would have had to straddle the pavement to get through. The front door stood two feet from the sidewalk at the top of three marble steps, with dips worn in their middle from eighty years of footsteps and repeated scrubbings. It opened onto a minuscule vestibule off a living room, after which came dining room and kitchen, all three no more than twelve feet by fourteen. There was a four-foot wide wooden stoop past the back door, two steps above a small concrete yard where clothes hung out to dry and children could play. A six-foot-high wooden fence enclosed the yard.

Nothing hung on the walls: there were no bookcases, no books. There was no Victrola. But there was a large console three-band radio which could receive short-wave broadcasts from Europe. The house was always spotless, sparsely furnished, lifeless. Two low rectangles projected from either party wall to separate the living from dining room; on each end of these little walls stood two decorative white wooden Doric columns pretending to hold the ceiling up and give a touch of class to what was in fact a clean brick shotgun shack.

We did not visit Fourth and Daly frequently. My mother was never keen to go, perhaps because she learned too little Yiddish after she married my father to make conversation easily, or perhaps because Mom had refused to speak to her until after I was born. (My maternal grandmother had been Italian;

hence my mother was a Gentile according to Jewish law.)[7] But while *Zaida* was alive we always went for Seder dinner on the first night of *Pesach*,[8] the Jewish holiday commemorating the Exodus from Egypt. That tale had some heft when I was old enough to grasp it, a few years after the fall of Nazi Germany.

A year or two before *Zaida* died my brother and I, six and eight, were dropped off at their house early on Passover, to watch him and Mom prepare the Passover meal. Boredom soon set in, and *Zaida* led us out to the back stoop where he produced two blocks of grainy pine and proceeded to carve two *dreydles*, the four-sided spinning top which Jewish children have played with for centuries. He inscribed letters in Hebrew – the traditional *aleph*, *beth*, *gimmel*, *nun* – one on each dreydle side, with a hard pencil, and explained how each letter had a value, from zero to three, and that the side facing up when it came to rest represented how many nuts, pennies, etc. the spinner had to give the other player. Then he counted twenty hazelnuts apiece into our hands and set us gambling on the stoop while he went inside to help Mom.

Three things always happened at the Passover dinner. Someone spilled the wine on Mom's white lace tablecloth, producing a scramble for cold water and lemon juice; there was a fight during which *Zaida* had to restrain my father; and *Zaida* lingered

7. The Jews trace membership matrilineally.

8. Passover.

over the wicked son's role in answering The Four Questions.[9] They are the *raison d'être* for the Seder, a religious service-cum-dinner to celebrate and teach the story of the Jews' deliverance from Egypt. Shortly after the service begins, the youngest boy must ask, "Why is this night different from all others?", and the leader of the Seder will retell the story of the Exodus, the repeated experience of our wandering tribe's history.

Though *Zaida* wasn't a believer, he was an ethnic realist who wanted his grandchildren to understand that Jewish blood is a perfume that attracts murderers, a pheromone no soap can wash away. So he dwelt on the role of the second son, the wicked one, who asks, "What does this service mean to you?", implying he is different, he can be what he wants, that the Seder and his blood's history mean nothing to him. The answer ordained for this son is "It is because of what the Lord did for me, not for you" – meaning, had you been there you'd have been left to be killed.

Today the *dreydle Zaida* made for me lies on my desk in Cambridge, as it has lain on other desks in other cities, other countries down the years. I don't know what happened to the one he made for my brother, who was cremated, a Christian, in San Francisco in 2005.

9. *Der fier kashes.*

At Fourth and Daly my father, Joe everywhere else, was always *Yossela*, Joey. He was a thin, short man, five feet five, with intense blue eyes, dark skin and thick black hair. He could have passed for an Argentinian tangoist or a Mafia hitman; perhaps the latter image had attracted my mother to him. Broad thick shoulders, large hands and well-muscled legs perfectly suited the featherweight semi-pro boxer he became.

Lust and rage beset his every age. His fists rose at the slightest provocation against all comers and sometimes against me. Bullies and every form of authority were his favoured targets. A local teenager who had been tormenting him when he was ten was struck from behind with a lead pipe one winter night. When he came to in hospital several hours and sixteen stitches later, he could recall only that he was passing the Borts' house when something hit him. He gave little Joey no more trouble.

He hated bullies all his life. One Sunday driving home from the store Joe saw two bigger boys beating a smaller boy beside the SKF ball bearing factory. He hit the brakes, leapt out and knocked down both older boys, then waited till the victim took off.

The Depression scarred him. He was twelve when it began. There was little work for carpenters, and for a time Yossela stood on a street corner hawking apples with *Zaida*. But the family needed more money, so at thirteen he left school without completing eighth grade and found work in a butcher shop on Fourth Street, a mile north of Fourth and Daly. His older sister and both brothers, older and younger, all finished high school. My father regretted his lack of formal education, because he thought that deficiency denied him the chance to make more money.

Yossela spent part of his first pay check on a new pair of shoes. *Zaida* beat him when he turned over that first week's earnings minus the cost of the shoes. The legend was his father's belt struck him so hard there were bloodstains from his ass on the ceiling.

Jewish boys undergo two rituals: circumcision at birth, about which they remember nothing, and, at thirteen, bar mitzvah, when they are called on a Saturday morning to read a passage from the Torah before the congregation as part of a rite admitting them to Jewish manhood. A celebration follows, however small, for family and friends. My father left *schul* immediately after his bar mitzvah, changed his clothes and went straight to work, Saturday being the busiest business day of the retail week.

Ninth and Race

Prostitution, gambling, fencing, contract murder, loan-sharking, political corruption and crime of every sort were the daily trade in Philadelphia's

Tenderloin, the oldest part of town. The Kevitch family ruled this stew for half a century, from Prohibition to the rise of Atlantic City. My mother was a Kevitch.

Not all Jewish boys become doctors, lawyers, violinists and Nobelists: some sons of immigrants from the Pale became criminals, often as part of or in cahoots with Italian crime families. A recent history calls them "tough Jews":[10] men like Meyer Lansky and Bugsy Siegel, who organized and ran Murder Incorporated for Lucky Luciano in the 'Twenties and 'Thirties, and Arnold Rothstein, better known as Meyer Wolfsheim in *The Great Gatsby*, who fixed the 1919 baseball World Series. The Kevitch family were tough Jews.

Their headquarters during the day was Milt's Bar and Grill at Ninth and Race, the heart of the Tenderloin, two miles north of Fourth and Daly. At night one or more male clan members supervised the family's "after-hours club" a few blocks away. We called Milt's Bar The Taproom and the after hours club The Club.

The Taproom stood alone between two vacant lots carpeted with broken bricks and brown beer bottle shards. Bums, beggars, prostitutes, stray cats and dogs peopled the surrounding streets; the smell of cat and human piss was always detectable, mixed

10. Rick Cohen, *Tough Jews*, Simon and Schuster, 1998.

with smoke from cigarette and cigar butts smouldering on the pavement. Milt's was a rectangular two-story building sixty feet long and eighteen feet wide. It fronted on the cobbles of Ninth Street and, through the back door, onto a cobbled alley. Both front and back doors were steel; the back door was never locked. The front window was glass block, set in The Taproom's brown brick facade like a glass eye in an old soldier's face. It could stop a fairly large calibre bullet and the wan light filtering through it brightened only the first few feet of the bar, the rest of which was too dark to make out faces.

More warehouse than pub, The Taproom served no food and little liquor. It was dank and smelled of stale beer, with too few customers to dispel either. I never saw more than a rummy or two drinking, or in the evenings perhaps a few sailors and a whore. The bar, with maybe a dozen stools, ran from the front door for a school bus's length towards the rear. Three plain iron tables stood near the back door with two iron chairs each. One of these tables stood beside a large colourful Wurlitzer jukebox that played only when a Kevitch – Abe, Big Milt, Meyer or Albert – sat there to talk with someone. On those occasions one had to wonder how the two men heard each other and why their table was placed so close to the Wurlitzer it drowned them out.

I never visited The Club, which began life as a "speakeasy" during Prohibition. My mother's father, Milton or Big Milt (to distinguish him from his nephew, Little Milt) and his brother Abe owned The Club and a nearby illegal still. "G-men", i.e. federal Treasury agents, raided the still one day, razed it and dumped its barrels of illegal alcohol in the gutters of the Tenderloin. Abe and Big Milt stood in the crowd as their hooch went down the drain and cheered the G-men on, as upright citizens should. The Kevitch family owned The Club for years after Big Milt and Abe died.

Big Milt was a Republican state legislator elected consistently for decades to represent the Tenderloin ward, which continued to vote ninety percent Republican for many years after the rest of the city went Democratic. It moved into the Democratic camp by a similar ninety per cent margin after the Kevitch family struck a deal with the Democratic leadership in the early 1950s. I had little contact with Big Milt, a distant figure who drove a black Lincoln Continental his state salary could not have paid for. He did not like my name and preferred to call me Donald. One birthday present from him of a child's camp chair had Donald stencilled across its canvas back. He handled what might politely be called governmental relations for the family and died in The Club one night, aged sixty-seven, of a massive lung haemorrhage brought on by tuberculosis.

His brother Abe headed the Kevitch family and ran the "corporation", the family loan-sharking business, along with the numbers bank,[11] gambling, fencing, prostitution and protection. When I got into trouble with the police as a teenager, Uncle Abe told me what to say to the judge at my hearing and what the judge would do, then sat in the back of the courtroom as the judge gave me a second chance and I walked without a record. Abe sat on a folding canvas chair in front of The Taproom in good weather with a cigar in his mouth. Men came up to him from time to time to talk, and sometimes they would go inside to the table beside the jukebox and talk while the music played. Inclement days and winters found him behind the bar. All serious family matters were referred to Abe until he retired and Meyer, the elder of his two sons, took over.

Meyer always greeted me with "Hello shit ass" when my mother took us to The Taproom for a visit. In good weather he sat on the same chair outside the bar his father had, and had the same conversations beside the jukebox. But unlike Abe, he did not live in the Tenderloin, his Italian wife wore minks and diamonds, and his son attended college before becoming a meat jobber with lucrative routes that dwindled after his father died. Also unlike Abe,

11. See "Numbers game", retrieved from Wikipedia 11 November 2012 (Wikipedia.org/wiki/Numbers game).

Meyer travelled, to Cuba before Castro, to Las Vegas and, in the 1970s, Atlantic City.

My father began playing in a local poker game and on his first two visits won rather a lot of money. The men running the game knew he was married to Meyer's cousin. They complained to Meyer that they could not continue to let Joe win and Meyer told my father not to play there again. The game was fixed. Joe ignored him. At his next session they cleaned him out.

Meyer had a surprising reach. Joe briefly owned a meat business with a partner, Marty.[12] It did well for eighteen months, the partners quarrelled bitterly, and Joe bought Marty out. A year later agents from the Internal Revenue Service (IRS) criminal division began investigating my father's affairs to discover whether he had been evading taxes by not reporting cash sales, which he and many other owners of cash businesses in the Fifties certainly had done. The agents were getting closer and jail loomed.

Joe spoke to Meyer, who told him several days later, "Joe, it'll cost $10,000," a large sum then and one Joe couldn't raise. Meyer suggested he ask his ex-partner to pay half since the IRS audit covered the partnership years. Marty told my father, "I'll give it to you when you need it for bread for your kids." Joe reported this to Meyer, but the price re-

12. See page 78.

mained $10,000. Joe put a second mortgage on our house which Abe co-signed, paid Meyer, and three days later the IRS agent called and said, "Mr Burt, I don't know who you know, and I don't know how you did it, but I've had a call from the IRS National Office in Washington, DC, ordering me to close this case in one week."

A year later the IRS criminal investigators returned, this time to audit Marty. Nothing Marty's tax lawyers could do put them off. He begged Joe to ask Meyer for help. But this time Meyer said there was nothing he could do. Marty endured a long trial which ended in a hung jury. Before the IRS could retry him he dropped dead of a heart attack; he was forty-six.

My mother's brother, Albert, was a taciturn man. He lived with his wife, Babe (neé Marian D'Orazio), and their four girls in a row home at 24th and Snyder in South Philadelphia's Italian neighborhood. He had no son. Babe was a great beauty, hence the nickname which she still bears proudly at ninety-two, and her daughters were beautiful as well. From the street their house looked like any other working-class row home in the neighbourhood, but inside it brimmed with toys, televisions, clothes and delicacies; the daughters were pampered and much envied. Education for Uncle Al, Aunt Babe and their daughters stopped with South Philly high. They attended neither church nor synagogue. There were no books on their tables or art on their walls, except a mural of a bucolic Chinese landscape in their living room.

Uncle Al was a detective on the Vice Squad, the Philadelphia police department's special unit charged with reducing prostitution, gambling, loansharking, fencing, protection and other rackets. The opportunities for corruption were many; some said the Vice Squad's function was to protect vice. Clarence Ferguson was the head of the Vice Squad. Babe's sister was Ferguson's wife.

We went to visit Uncle Al's house one Sunday when I was ten. A week before, Billy Meade, the boss of the Republican machine in Philadelphia, had been shot and nearly killed in The Club. He was drinking in the early hours at his accustomed spot at the bar when someone shot him with a silenced pistol shoved through the inspection grill in the door when it was slid aside in answer to a knock. The shooter was short, he stood on a milk crate to fire through the grill, and must have known Meade could be found in The Club in the wee hours of Sunday morning and where along the bar he customarily stood.

Billy Meade and Big Milt, Uncle Al's father, were on the outs at the time and Meade had done something that caused Big Milt real trouble. Uncle Al was just five foot five, had ample experience with and access to firearms, and would have known Meade frequented The Club. I watched the police take Uncle Al from his house that morning and confiscate a large chest containing his sword and gun collection. He was tried but not convicted because the weapon used was never found and Babe said he had been making love to her in their marriage bed when the shooting occurred. No one else was accused of the attempted murder, and when Meade recovered he made peace with Big Milt. They both died of natural causes.

Some years later Uncle Al was again involved in a shooting. This time there was no question that he was the shooter. He had stopped for a traffic-light in a rough neighbourhood on the way home from work. Four young black men approached his car. According to Al they intended to car-jack him. I never saw Uncle Al without his gun, a .38 police revolver he wore in a holster on his belt. When he drove he always unholstered the gun and laid it on the seat beside him. One of the men tried to open the driver's door and Uncle Al grabbed his gun from the seat and shot through the window, seriously wounding him. The other three fled and Al chased them, firing as he went. He brought down a second and the other two were picked up by the police a short time later.

The papers were full of pictures of the car's shattered windows, the two black casualties and the white off-duty detective who had shot them. The police department commended him for bravery. I never saw Uncle Al angry; crossed, he stared at you coolly with diamond blue eyes and sooner or later, inevitably, evened the score and more.

All the Kevitch men of my grandfather's and mother's generation had mistresses and did not disguise the fact. Their wives and all the mistresses were Gentiles, excepting Abe's wife, Annie. Uncle Al had a passion for Italian women and consorted openly with his Italian mistress for the last twenty-five years of his life. Divorce was not unheard of in the family, but Al died married to Babe.

One of Uncle Al's daughters described her father by saying "He collected." The things he collected included antique swords, guns, watches and jewellery, as well as delinquent principal and interest on extortionate loans the family "corporation" made; protection money from shopkeepers, pimps, madams, numbers writers, gambling dens, thieves and racketeers; and gifts from the Philadelphia branch of the Gambino Mafia family run by Angelo "the gentle don" Bruno. Joe and Uncle Al died within months of each other, and at Joe's funeral Babe proudly told me how Al would make the more difficult collections, say from a gambler who refused to pay his debts. He would cradle his .38 in the flat of his hand and curl his thumb through the trigger guard to hold it in place, so it became a second palm. Then he'd slap the delinquent hard in the head with his blue steel palm. His collection record was quite good.

Angelo Bruno and Uncle Al were close for years, until Bruno was killed in 1980 at the age of sixty-nine by a shotgun blast to the back of his head. Albert had protected him and his lieutenants from arrest. In exchange Bruno contributed to Uncle Al's collections. Uncle Al often told his daughters what a wonderful, decent, kind man Bruno was and that he did not allow his family to deal in drugs. The Albert Kevitch family held the Don in high regard.

Babe adored her husband and my four cousins adored their father. They were grateful for the luxurious lives he gave them and proud of the fear he inspired. No one bullied them. Babe called the four girls together before they went to school the day the newspapers broke the story of Al's arrest on suspicion of shooting Billy Meade and told them if anyone asked whether the Al Kevitch suspected of the shooting was their father they should hold their heads up and answer "Yes".

My mother, Louise Kevitch, Albert's younger sister, was born to Milton and Anita Kevitch (née Anita Maria Pellegrino) a block or two from The Taproom in 1917. Nine months later my maternal grandmother, Anita, a Catholic, died in the 1918 flu epidemic and her children, Louise and Albert, were taken in by their Italian immigrant grandmother, who lived nearby. She raised Louise from the age of two until thirteen in an apartment over her candy store, its profits more from writing numbers than selling sweets. Louise was thirteen when her grandmother died; she lived with Uncle Abe and Aunt Annie in their large house across the street from The Taproom from then until, at twenty-one, she married my father.

Louise graduated from William Penn High School in central Philadelphia, wore white gloves out and about and shopping in the downtown department stores, went to the beauty parlour once a week and had a "girl", a black maid, three days a week to clean and iron, a luxury that Joe could ill afford. She did not help him in the store. She spoke reverentially of her brother, Al, and his role as a detective on the Vice Squad, of Big Milt, who worked in Harrisburg, and of Uncle Abe and the family "corporation", which would help us should we need it. Meyer was Lancelot to her, though we never quite knew why. Louise constantly invoked the principle of "family" as a mystic bond to be honored with frequent visits to The Taproom and the Kevitches. Joe did all he could to keep us from their ambit. It was a child-rearing battle he won, but not decisively. Louise kept trying to force us closer to her family; they fought about it for fifty-three years.

My mother never *bentsch licht*[13] or went to *schul*, except on the high holidays, Rosh Hashana[14] and Yom Kippur.[15] She never told us her mother and grandmother were Italian. When Babe revealed the secret to me, Louise didn't speak to her for months. We never knew her father had married another Gentile shortly after her mother (Anita) died, and fathered aunts and uncles we never met. She never mentioned Big Milt's mistress, Catherine, who was with him at his death. She never explained how four families – Abe and Annie, Meyer's, his brother Milton's first and second ones – lived well on earnings of what appeared to be a failing bar and after-hours club in the red-light district. Why her brother was so important if he was only a detective, how his family lived so well on a detective's salary – these were never explained. She did not tell us her mink coat was a gift from her brother, or how he came by it. Any questions about what Uncle Al or Meyer actually did, any suggestion that any Kevitch male was less than a gentleman infuriated her, brought slaps or punishment, and went unanswered. We learned about the Kevitches from observation, from what they told us, and from the papers.

13. The woman's Hebrew blessing of the Sabbath candles as she lights them.
14. Jewish New Year.
15. Day of Atonement.

CHILDHOOD'S HOUSES

716 South Fourth

My parents' marriage was a bare-knuckle fight to the death. The early rounds were fought at 716 South Fourth Street, roughly equidistant from Fourth and Daly and Ninth and Race, where I lived from a few days after birth in 1942 till nearly five. I watched the next fifteen rounds from a seat at 5141 Whitaker Avenue in the Feltonville section of North Philadelphia, where we moved in 1947. The match continued after I left.

Joe and Louise were introduced through mutual friends at a "clubhouse" in South Philadelphia that he and other bachelor friends rented to drink, throw parties and take their girl friends to "make out". Respectable lower-middle-class girls in the late 1930s did not allow themselves to be "picked up", nor did they copulate till married and then not often. Louise and her girlfriends lived in the Tenderloin, which made their virtue suspect even as it conferred allure. But there was no question Louise Kevitch, Al's sister and Big Milt's daughter, took her maidenhead intact to the wedding sheets: a gynaecologist had to remove it surgically after my parents tried and failed for several days to consummate their marriage. This difficulty was a harbinger of my mother's enduring distaste for sex.

She was a quite attractive woman at twenty when they met and, shortly thereafter, married: five foot, a hundred pounds, brown eyes, slim, with good breasts and fine legs, long soft brown hair and the hauteur of someone with roots to hide who sniffed at anything or anyone not quite *comme il faut*. But Louise was unacceptable to grandmother Rose Bort because she was not Jewish, if not for other reasons. Louise would not consider converting. Rose did not attend their wedding.

The waves of Ashkenazim from the Pale who came to Philadelphia from the 1880s through the early 1920s settled near Fourth Street in South Philadelphia. Louise, or Lou as my father called her, went to live with her husband above Joe's Meat Market, the "Store", at 716, in the heart of the cobbled South Fourth Street shopping district. Their home was the top two floors of a three-storey, forty-five by fourteen-foot brown brick late Victorian building with a coal furnace. The ground or "first" floor was the Store. A refrigerated meat case extended some twenty feet from the front display window, also refrigerated, to a small area holding basic dry goods: black-eyed peas, lima beans, rice, Bond bread, Carnation canned milk, Campbell soups, tea, Maxwell House ground coffee in airtight tin cans and sugar. The next fifteen feet contained a small cutting room, the "back room", with two butcher blocks, hot and cold water taps and a fifty-gallon galvanized iron drum for washing platters. Behind the cutting room was a ten-by-twelve walk-in ice box where rump and rounds of beef, pork loins, frying chickens and smoked meats waited to be cut up and put on sale in the window or the case. A decoratively stamped tin ceiling ran from the front door to the ice box. I came to live two floors above Joe's Meat Market three days after I was born.

The Store's front door was almost entirely plate glass, so that customers could see we were open if the door was closed; but, to avoid missing a sale, it almost never was. A screen door was hung in summer to keep out flies. Two-thirds of the way down the Store, adjacent to the wall – opposite the meat case – was a trapdoor that opened on rickety steps down to the coal-bin and furnace in the cellar. The cellar also held fifty-pound sacks of rice, cartons of sugar, and other goods, along with the rats and roaches that fed on them. You had to tend the furnace once in the middle of the night or the fire would go out. Once out it was hard to rekindle.

Behind the case ran the counter on which meat was wrapped, chopped, cut, or piled while serving a customer. Bags in sizes that held from two to twenty-five pounds were stacked beneath the counter in vertical piles divided by wooden dowels. Midway down the counter was the register, which only my father was allowed to open. On a nail under the register hung a loaded .38-calibre revolver and a black jack on a leather strap; a baseball bat leaned against the back wall by the cosh. All three were used at one time or another.

Three scales trisected the top of the refrigerated case. One-pound cardboard boxes of lard for sale were stacked two feet high on either side of the scale's weighing pans, making it impossible to see the meat being weighed on them. The butcher slid a box of lard onto the scale as he placed the meat on it and stood back in a "Look Ma, no hands" pose so the customer could see him. Slabs of fat back, salt pork and bacon also stood in piles on enamelled platters atop the case. Towards the end of the day in summer, beads of grease dripped from these piles onto the platters. Flies were everywhere, more in summer than winter, but always there.

Out the door next left was a poulterer's where chickens, ducks and turkeys in cages squawked, honked and gobbled, and the stink of rotten eggs and ammonia from fowl-shit mixed with sawdust drifted onto the street. These birds were awaiting death and let every passerby know it. To the right was a yarn shop and next to it, on the corner, the fish store. The odour of rotting fish heads, tails, scales and blood rose from a garbage can beneath the filleting block, stronger on busier days than slow. Carp milled in galvanized tubs, finning and thrashing until

Mr Segal, the fishmonger, thrust his hand among them and snatched the one the customer pointed to. A brief commotion as he yanked it from the tub, then with his left arm he held it still on the chopping block while his right hand severed head and tail with one blow each. Mr Segal's right arm, the one that held the machete-sized beheading knife, was much thicker than his left, the result of dispatching fish Mondays through Saturdays. My father's right arm and shoulder were similarly muscled from cutting meat.

Pushcarts lined the curbs for blocks like huge wheelbarrows, their rear two spoke wheels four feet in diameter, the front wheel a third that, with long shafts extending from the barrow, as if for horses. The carts rested on their smaller front wheels with the shafts angled skywards during business hours. They clogged the street so that there was just enough

4th south of Bainbridge, looking north towards the Store, 1940s

room for a single file of cars or a trolley to pass, and fouled the curb with the smell of rotting tomatoes, cabbage leaves and onions. In winter rusty fifty-five-gallon oil drums stood between some of the push-carts with trash fires burning in them all day. The pushcart vendors stood round them for warmth until a customer appeared.

Mr Drucker, a tall, thin kindly-looking man, sold fruit and vegetables from his pushcart in front of the yarn store, and smiled at me and asked "*Nu, Danela?*"[16] as I toddled by. He was there Monday to Saturday, no matter how hot or cold, and always wore a cloth flat cap. He could have been a pedlar in Lvov. At night Mr Drucker closed up shop by levering onto the cart's shafts so that his weight brought the front wheel off the cobbles as his feet hit the ground and the cart balanced on its two large wheels. Then with a heave he swung it from the curb, negotiated the trolley tracks, and slowly pushed it round the corner and down three blocks to the pushcart garage where he locked it up for the night. The pushcarts, with their high wooden sides, steel rimmed wooden wheels and goods, were heavy and didn't roll well. Moving them was a job for a horse, but Mr Drucker had no horse.

16. 'What's up, Danny?'

Fourth Street was declining as a Jewish shopping district when my father bought the Store in 1940. Jewish immigration from the Pale had been choked off in the 1920s by the new US quota system and the diminishing anti-Semitism that accompanied the first stages of Bolshevism in Russia. The first Jewish generation born in Philadelphia prospered and promptly moved to better neighbourhoods in Northeast and West Philadelphia. Poor blacks from the southern states took their places and with them came poverty, different foods, more alcohol, different violence, different street crime and prejudice. Rye bread, pickles, herring and corned beef gave way to hominy grits, collard greens, catfish and chitlins, the odour of garlic and cumin replaced by the barbecue tang of wood smoke mixed with pig fat. At New Year's Joe's Meats had wooden barrels four feet high and three wide with mounds of smoked hog jaws for sale, bristles and teeth still intact. This ghoulish food, roasted for hours with black-eyed peas and collard greens, was the traditional New Year's turkey for Southern field hands, and was supposed to bring luck.

There was a bar across the street and two hundred feet north of the Store, at the corner of Fourth and Bainbridge. Payday was Friday. Friday and Saturday nights the sirens would wail their way to that bar; sometimes screams or shots were heard. Knife fights and back-alley crap games that ended in violence were common. Many customers on Saturday and Sunday mornings were hung-over, and it was not unusual for the men to sport freshly bandaged hands and heads. Joe sometimes ate lunch at Pearl's, a small luncheonette round the corner from the Store. One Sunday we were sitting on stools at Pearl's counter eating lunch when a young black man said something which led him, his companion and Joe to walk outside and square up. The tough pulled a nine-inch switch blade. Joe crouched, called him a nigger motherfucker and beat him bloody.

Joe's Meat Market would have failed ten years earlier than it did but for the coming of war. The US Navy Yard at the foot of Broad Street, four miles southeast of William Penn's hat, was working three shifts a day when the Japanese attacked Pearl Harbour on December 7, 1941. Local woollen mills, machine shops, and foundries soon followed suit. They drew labourers, many of them black, to the city; any capable man or woman in South Philadelphia who wanted steady work at good wages had it, including some of my relatives. And these workers bought their meat at Joe's. For the first time my father was making more than a living.

The US government rationed meats and staples like coffee and sugar, which spawned a black market. They created a federal agency, the Office of Price Administration (OPA), with inspectors to police the ration system and prevent profiteering; this drove black market prices higher. Joe struck a deal with a black market slaughterhouse to assure his supply of meat. He fetched it from the slaughterer's at night in a Chevy panel truck and unloaded it himself. Word got round that you could always get plenty of pork chops and roasts at Joe's without ration coupons.

Whitey, an OPA inspector in his fifties, nearly six-foot tall, fat and officious, walked into the Store one Saturday morning when it was packed with customers come to buy meat without ration coupons. If anyone asked the price of a cut the butcher called out "Next!" and she left meatless. Whitey asked to see the ration coupons for what was being sold.

South Philadelphia's ghettos – Jewish, Italian, Irish, Black – produced many good semi-pro boxers. Joe was one of them. He was twenty-nine, fast, with an Eastern European peasant's arms and shoulders thickened from butchering; he could take a punch. He had little respect for authority, a Depression era fear of anything that threatened his living, and an uncontrollable temper. Joe asked Whitey to come back on Monday when the weekend rush was over. Whitey asked again. Joe came from behind the counter, faced him and told him to come back another day. Whitey started to shut the front door saying he would order the Store closed if Joe didn't show him the coupons. Joe knocked him through the front door's plate glass.

The Kevitch family lawyer defended Joe at his

trial, which Uncle Abe attended to see justice done. When Whitey was called to the stand he rose, looked at Uncle Abe and said, "Abe, if my dead mother got up from her grave and begged, I wouldn't lift a finger to help that kid of yours," then testified as damningly as he could. My father did not go to jail. He paid a modest fine; business went on as usual.

Joe began to teach his wife to drive shortly after they married. Those days trolleys ran frequently along the steel tracks in front of 716 South Fourth. The pre-war family coupé had a manual clutch and gearshift which Louise found difficult to master. She began to pull away from the curb one Sunday afternoon, my father in the passenger seat instructing, and stalled on the tracks. She flooded the carburettor trying to restart the car, while a trolley, bell clanging, stopped inches from the coupé's back bumper. The starter turned the engine over futilely while the conductor continued to ring his bell. After a minute he leaned from his window and cursed Louise, her sex, her intelligence and her parents. The passenger door flew open and Joe ran to the trolley car, pried open the front double doors, dragged the conductor from the car and knocked him out. The conductor lay still on the cobbles. My father walked back to the car, got behind the wheel, started it and drove away.

A few days before Christmas 1946 Joe won $250[17] in a crap game and blew it all on two sets of O-Gauge Lionel model electric trains, passenger and freight, for my brother and me. Lionel did not manufacture model trains during the war and the first postwar sets were in short supply and dear. The freight set's six-wheel-driver workhorse steam engine pulled a coal tender and silver Sunoco oil tanker, an orange boxcar with Baby Ruth logo, an operating black flatbed log car and a caboose. A sleek ten-wheel Pennsylvania Railroad passenger steam engine with tender rocketed three passenger cars and a club car round the layout, their windows lit by a bulb inside each car. Both engines puffed fake smoke when a white pellet dropped down their smokestacks melted on the hot headlight bulbs below. The whistle diaphragm was located in the tenders and activated by a button on a controller clipped to the track. Pressing a button on a remote-control track would trigger a plunger below the log car to tip the floor of the car up and dump the three logs it carried. Accessories included a gateman with a swinging lantern who popped out of his gatehouse when a train rolled over a nearby contact, a half-dozen street lights, and a transformer to run it all. Joe and a buddy sat on the floor in the front room above the Store that Christmas morning assembling

17. $2,500 in 2012 dollars.

track and wiring controllers. He ran those trains round whistling and smoking all Christmas day, and every Christmas after until I was twelve. My father had few toys as a child, and no trains. Sixty-five years later I still run them round at Christmas.

Early in 1946 slicing abdominal pains doubled Joe up, and doctors diagnosed acute Crohn's disease[18] or rotting guts – the consequence of Jewish genes, bad boyhood diet, and heavy smoking – shortly after I turned three. He left hospital six months later, a surviving experiment in radical intestinal resectioning: eighty-five pounds, short-gutted, and permanently diarrheoic. His bowels plagued him for the rest of his life: diarrhoea irritated his anus, and for years he drove sitting on an inflatable child's plastic swim-ring; there was talk of a colostomy, as he trudged from doctor to doctor seeking relief. His groans and diarrhoea-browned toilet bowls were a fixture in our house. Into my teens I was afraid he might die at any minute.

The famous surgeon who removed much of his rotted tripe, in the pioneering operation that saved his life, ordered him to convalesce and find a hobby. He went to Florida with Louise for his first ever vacation and there, as a form of therapy, began to fish from a Miami pier. By the time he returned from Florida he had his hobby. A diversion became

18. A chronic intestinal disease that ultimately blocks the bowels.

a passion, then an obsession and finally a calling: he died a charter-boat captain on the Jersey coast. But his bowels and stomach tortured him the remaining forty-nine years of his life; he developed stomach cancer at eighty which would have killed him had a heart attack not carried him off first.

5141 Whitaker Ave

Stacks of $20, $50 and $100 bills with rubber bands around them, the four-year fruits of war, covered the kitchen table on V-J Day, August 15, 1945, waiting to be hidden in a bank's safe-deposit box. One year later Joe returned from convalescing in Florida, thirty-two years old, with a newfound passion for salt-water sport fishing, an even chance he would die young, and memories of signs at southern hotels saying – "No jews or dogs allowed". It was the worst possible time to buy a house: demand penned by the war, servicemen returning with G.I. loans, and wartime dearth of construction combined to inflate prices. But for the first time in my father's life a pigmy front lawn, grassy side-plot in a private alleyway between the next row of two-storey houses, garage, basement with oak floors and a six-foot mahogany bar with three leather stools were his if he wanted them. Joe took some stacks from the safe-deposit box and bought an end-of-row house in Feltonville, a working and lower-middle class neighbourhood in north Philadelphia to which we moved a few months before my fifth birthday. The house was never worth as much as it was that spring of 1947, and my parents lost most of their investment in real terms when they sold it forty years later.

Joe often visited the "box" over the next eight years. War work dwindled and with it went Fourth Street's shoppers. Each month my parents spent more than the Store took in. Joe's innards continued to rot; his money worries worsened; Louise grew fat, and bickering became screaming matches, with fists slamming tables and smashed plates. But Joe's visits to the *Shvitz* – the local steam baths – each Monday of the year and fishing trips each Tuesday, March through mid-December, continued, as did Louise's "help", her weekly beauty parlour, and the family's annual two weeks at the "shore", whether Atlantic City or Long Beach Island. They borrowed money for emergencies and took the last cash stack from the "box" when I was twelve.

My parents used my fifth birthday to display their new house to the Burts and Kevitches. (When Uncle Bernie changed his name after the war from Jewish-sounding Bort to Waspier Burt to help his career as a lingerie buyer for a downtown department store, Joe followed suit.) The Burt family war hero, Uncle Moishe, showed up. So did his Kevitch counterpart, Uncle Milton. Both had served in the

Pacific, Milton as a military policeman, Moishe as a paratrooper. Milton brought home a Japanese rifle and malaria; Moishe, a chest of medals, a metal right arm and leg, chrome claw-hand and an addiction to morphine. He had charged and destroyed an enemy machine gun nest on Guadalcanal to earn medals, prostheses, pensions and federal benefits. Handsome, still dashing, Uncle Moishe married five times before he died, a successful chicken farmer, in Texas.

I met him for the first time that birthday and quickly told him about my Japanese rifle, which he asked to see. We went down to our basement and when I showed it to him he picked it up with hand and claw, made me promise not to tell anyone, then taught me how to make a bayonet thrust. I saw him once more a few years later at Fourth and Daly when Joe would have beat him senseless had my grandparents not managed to drag him away. Moishe, the youngest of their four children and Mom's favourite, had persuaded them to mortgage their house to fund his business deal. The deal, if there was a deal, went south, leaving Mom and Pop with a mortgage they couldn't pay, Pop dying and no other assets to speak of. We went to their house for my father to discuss what was to be done, but when he saw Moishe he lost his temper and punched him. I never saw or heard from Moishe again; he did not attend either of his parents' funerals, nor my father's. He had numerous children, my first cousins, whom I have never met and whose names I have never known.

The new house in Feltonville had a "breakfast room" where we ate at a table for six, separated by a half wall from a small kitchen, the last of five modest rooms on the first floor. Joe sat at the head of the table on the two or three nights a week when he was home early enough for us to eat as a family. If he was not present, his chair stayed empty, as did the large red plush armchair with thick feather-stuffed cushions in the living room. We were forbidden to sit in it after the cushions were plumped for his return from work.

There was no art, no pictures on the walls, no musical instruments. Volumes of *The Reader's Digest Condensed Book Club*, a set of *Encyclopaedia Britannica* and *The Naked and the Dead* stood on four shelves in the basement. Our periodicals were *Reader's Digest*, *Life*, *Look*, *Vogue* and *Salt Water Sportsman.* A television rested on the living room's wall-to-wall carpet. There was a large pre-war 78 Victrola cum radio with amber-coloured tuning face on a shelf in the basement above a small stack of "swing" and "big band" records from the 1940s, one of which contained Al Jolson singing "The Anniversary Waltz". The first two lines Jolson sang go: "Oh how we danced on the night we were wed / We vowed our true love though a word wasn't said", which Joe rendered in a loud baritone as "Oh how we danced on the night we were wed / I needed a wife like a hole in the head". Linoleum covered the breakfast room and kitchen floors.

The door slammed behind him when he came home and called out, "Lou, is dinner ready?" They did not greet each other, nor kiss, nor touch. I never saw them kiss. If dinner was late a fight would start. On five out of six work nights, Joe came home too late to eat with us and ate dinner alone, reading the paper. At breakfast he would go over yesterday's receipts and lists of provisions to be picked up at the wholesalers. When the family ate together he talked to his sons rather than his wife. If he spoke to her at table it was about how bad business had been that day or week or month. After dinner he flopped in his chair to read the paper, smoke a cigarette and doze. He went to bed around ten.

Louise did not go with him. She sat watching television in the living room, or in the kitchen talking on the telephone, drinking coffee, smoking and doodling on scraps of paper and newspaper margins. After half an hour he would call, "Lou, Lou, come to bed". Most mornings I found her asleep on the couch in the living room. They shared a bedroom, but she rarely slept there when he was in the bed. He was consistently unfaithful to her all their wedded life, either with whores or girlfriends. She set her brother to catch him in one suspected affair that worried her more than most. A scene followed; she presented the evidence in front of us children. He began to pack, she kept berating him, dishes flew, she threatened to call Uncle Al. Joe never hit her. In time their marriage decayed into indifference; his excuse for not leaving was "you kids", hers was, "how would I support myself" and "what would people say?"

The day began with screams and shouts. Our house had one bathroom, with tiled floor, single sink, shower and tub for the four of us, and a basement W.C. We had a washing machine and later a dryer, but clean clothes often shirked the climb from basement laundry room to bedrooms. Mornings were a scramble to empty bowels and bladders, find clean underwear and socks, and get to work or school; the house rang with cries of "Lou, where's my shorts" or "Mom, I need socks". Yesterday's dinner dishes tilted at odd angles in a yellow rubber-coated drying rack by the kitchen sink, where unwashed pots with congealed rice or potatoes were piled.

Pop died in 1954 and Mom turned her *kvetching* (corrosive whining) on her children and their wives. She always worried about money – though between her social security checks and her children's help she had more than enough – and used a "limited" phone service. This allowed her two free calls a day for a nominal fee. She husbanded her free calls for "emergencies" and signalled with two rings when she wanted family to call her. Her signals became a ukase, ignored at your peril. Almost every evening before Joe came home, while Louise struggled with supper, Mom signalled. Apparently bearing two sons, time, and an old widow's loneliness had cleansed the *shiksa* from Louise's blood. If she didn't ring back immediately Mom would use one of her "emergency" calls to complain to Joe when he came home from work. Dinner was never on time; asked when it would be ready Louise snapped "When I say so". We ate hostage to the signal. Mom died at ninety-nine and lived alone until her death.

The neighbourhood was about sixty percent Gentile and forty percent Jewish when we moved there, but the Jews were leaving for the suburbs. It was seventy percent Gentile by the time I was twelve and today is an Hispanic section of Philadelphia's inner city. The Catholic kids mostly went to Saint Ambrose parochial school on Roosevelt Boulevard. Saint Ambrose was attached to a large Catholic church in the next block west from our synagogue. Fights with the Saint Ambrosians were a staple of Jewish high holy days. It was generally accepted that the Gentile boys, the *shkutz*, were tougher than the Jewish, with a few exceptions.

Non-Catholics attended Creighton Elementary, the local public primary school, teaching grades kindergarten through eighth. It was a five-storey ochre brick building set on a third of a city block. An adjoining concrete schoolyard and a gravel playing field occupied the rest. Six-foot-high pointy iron palings set three inches apart formed a palisade from the school's north facade round the cement school yard and gravel ball field to the building's south facade. There were heavy steel mesh grills painted off-white on the ground level windows. It looked like a prison. The gates were locked from 4 p.m. to 7.30 a.m. the next morning. There was an assembly hall where every morning we said a prayer, pledged the flag and heard a reading from the Bible, mostly from the New Testament; an oak-floored gym half again the size of a basketball court, with several vaulting horses, sweat-grey tattered tumbling mats, rings, ceiling-high climbing ropes, and basketball hoops at either end; a wood shop where sixth, seventh and eighth grade boys learned to handle the tools they would need for adult jobs and made "zip guns"; and a "Home Ec" room with stoves, refrigerators and sewing machines where girls learned the skills of their sex. Thanksgiving, Christmas and Easter were the big holidays, with paper turkeys, crèches, dyed eggs, bunnies and baskets in profusion. Few Old Creightonians went to college.

Our neighbourhood was eight blocks long and four deep, bounded on the north by the Boulevard, east by railroad tracks, south by a creek where we trapped tadpoles and west by the Boulevard again. It supported eleven "mom and pop" stores on eleven corners: two groceries, two kosher butchers, two candy stores, a corner drug store, barber shop, beauty parlour, shoe repair and Polan's, a luncheonette. The northeastern US headquarters of catalogue retailer Sears & Roebuck, with a two-square-block, three-storey department store attached, was four blocks away across the Boulevard. The department store entrance housed a popcorn machine and clerk selling large bags of it for 15¢. A baseball, knife, deflated football or basketball fit neatly below the popcorn at the bottom of one of these bags, and the advent of spring and fall found groups of boys wandering the sporting goods aisles munching popcorn and looking out for store detectives.

We played on Whitaker Avenue's wide asphalt street, a six-blocks-long dead end. There were no parks or playgrounds. Boys played *stick ball* with a cut-off broom handle for bat and a hollow rubber ball two and a quarter inches in diameter; *half-ball* with the same bat but with the ball cut in half and inverted so it looked like a deep saucer and dipped, curved and floated unpredictably when properly pitched; and *hose-ball*, again with the same broom-handle bats, and four-inch hose lengths cut from rubber garden hoses. Sensible neighbours kept their brooms and hoses inside from Easter until the players had stolen enough for the coming season.

The street game from September till Christmas was rough-touch American football. Participants left these games cut and bruised from slamming into parked cars and curbs, sometimes with sprains, occasionally with a broken bone. The parked cars did not fare well either. There was a stop sign where a side street from the Boulevard intersected Whitaker Avenue. Joe drove down that street every day coming home from work, but never stopped. The neighbours cursed him.

Competition from the national food chains (A&P and Food Fair), along with the Jewish exodus, slowly throttled the local stores, except for Polan's, where the Jewish *gonifs*[19] hung out. Every Monday night between 7 and 8 they gathered to settle the weekend's gambling debts. Accounts were squared when "Fats", a 350-pound man in his late thirties, and his two bodyguards drove off in his white Cadillac convertible. One afternoon drink-fuelled insults – kike and sheeny – from mourners at an Irish wake a few doors along from Polan's led to shoving, a *hey rube!* and brawl, followed by police and ambulances. The guys who hung out at Polan's were not sissies, and the grade-school boys there eating hamburgers and fries looked up to them.

19. Thieves or hustlers.

Joe worked six and a half days a week, fishing and *Schvitz* his only recreations. The Store was open every day except for national holidays like Christmas and Easter Sunday, and he had only one helper. He was too tired or worried to talk much when he came home from work; he never encouraged his sons to become butchers. During our two-week holiday at the "shore" in August he arrived from Philadelphia late on Sunday night, spent Monday afternoon with us on the beach and returned to Philadelphia after fishing Tuesday. The one vacation he took was a fishing trip to Cape Hatteras, North Carolina, for channel bass, five years after his convalescence, with me along.

Hatteras is ten hours southeast by car and ferry from Philadelphia. We arrived at a motel near Ocracoke Inlet, North Carolina, at two in the morning in the middle of a nor'easter. It was still blowing hard four hours later when we woke to seas too rough to fish. A grand old wooden resort hotel just opening for the season was recommended for breakfast. There was one table in use in the otherwise closed dining room. We were seated with another party of breakfasting fishermen from Philadelphia at the long table; Joe knew one of them. A tall, courtly, white-haired black waiter was serving. He took our order, and ham, bacon, eggs arrived with large sides of hominy grits: a ground maize porridge served slathered in butter, and a staple of Southern breakfasts.

North Carolina had been a slave state and a lynchpin of the Confederacy. Segregation – *de jure* and *de facto* – was the iron rule in 1952, two years before the US Supreme Court ruled that segregated schooling was illegal. The Klan was large and powerful; there were separate toilets, restaurants, water fountains and motels for blacks and whites, and blacks rode at the back of the bus. Jews were not popular.

The other party finished before us and one of them called to the waiter, "Boy! Boy! Cum y'ere" in an ersatz, mocking, field-hand's patois from *Gone With The Wind*. The waiter approached: "Yes sir, can I help you?" The man replied "Boy, dem's was rail fahn grits. Why's, dey's de bestest grits ah evah did have! Could ah's hav'es some more of dem dere grits?" The waiter said, "I'm glad you liked them sir. I'll check with the kitchen". The bigot sat down, smirking, and the waiter headed for the kitchen. My father rose, plate in hand, before the waiter took two steps, walked round and scraped his grits onto the man's plate, saying "Here, you want some more grits?" Joe stood over him while the man ate the grits; the waiter looked on from the side of the room.

Joe did only two things religiously: he fished each Tuesday from March till mid-December and he went to *Schvitz* on Mondays. His ageing mother he saw once or twice a month when her nagging made him feel guilty; visited his brother-in-law with the family at Christmas; met cousins-in-law if there was a problem or at a crap game; went to a movie, dinner or family celebration three or four times a year with his wife; and worked the rest of the time. His stomach troubles had stopped his serious drinking in 1947, and he generally whored discreetly.

The *Schvitz*, the Camac Baths, was a three-storey building half-a-block square, built almost to the curb on Camac Street, an alley eight minutes walk southeast from City Hall. A clerk stood behind a desk in the small foyer, in front of rows of steel lock-boxes with keys on elastic wristbands hanging from their little doors, behind which steel trays a foot long with two-inch-high sides rested in cubbyholes. The clerk handed Joe a tray for valuables as he signed in. Joe always carried a wad of cash two or three inches thick, which he placed with his wallet and Timex in the tray, then watched the clerk lock it in its cubbyhole. The clerk handed him the key to the lock-box, a bed sheet and paper bath shoes, and he went through another door on his right into the locker room.

The locker room, a well lighted forty-foot-square space smelling of linament and disinfectant, had a tiled floor and several hundred sheet-metal hanging lockers arranged in facing rows of thirty with benches between. There was a barber shop, shoeshine stand, cafeteria, and "sun room" for tanning. Bathers undressed, draped the sheet over themselves like togas, shouted "locker" for an attendant to lock up their clothes, and shuffled through another door and down a staircase to the baths. Along the far perimeter of the basement that housed the baths were two twelve-by-eighteen-foot white-tiled hot rooms behind a plate glass door; towel-draped deckchairs lined their walls. The temperature in one was 125 degrees; in the other, 150 degrees Fahrenheit. A ten-by-ten foot steam room reeking of pine adjoined the cooler hot room. Marble benches lined its walls and there was a cold shower in the corner for bathers to cool down, so as to prolong the time they could bear the steam.

At the other end of the baths was the *platza* room where the *platza* man, naked except for a black canvas loin cloth, cold water coursing down him from a hose stuffed under a floppy canvas hat he wore, rubbed bathers down with soapy brushes fashioned from eucalyptus leaves. Joe always took a *platza*. He would lie on the highest of the room's three oak racks with a canvas hat fished from a bucket of cold water on his head, Willie, the *platza*-man, six-foot-one and a good 230 pounds, looming over him. Willie controlled the heat from a lever under the second level of benches; each time he depressed it the room got hotter. Joe viewed a *platza* as a contest between him and Willie to see who would quit first. Willie had the advantage of standing in the cold water shower from the hose under his hat and could give *platzas* for hours. He would bear down on bathers with the brush – massaging, washing and cooking them at the same time. Every three or four minutes he would ratchet up the heat, and once in a while take the hose from under his hat and sprinkle their most tender parts, like the backs of calves, with cold water. Joe outlasted anyone else taking a platza when he took his; once even Willie wilted.

Finished, Willie helped bathers down from the *platza* bench and into the stall immediately outside for a cold shower. He handed favourites a shot of bourbon from a pint-bottle secreted in the *platza* room and then they went for their "sheet wrap". Twelve or so deckchairs stood along rails forming a twelve-by-twelve foot square between the *platza* and hot rooms. An attendant covered a deckchair with towels and a sheet, and bathers reclined in it. He laid towels across their chests, legs and arms, swathed heads and necks in more towels, then wrapped the sheet around them like tinfoil round a roast. There they lay, sweating and dozing or talking to other shrouded men.

The Camac Baths transplanted to America an Eastern European ritual from the Pale. Camac's mid-century habitués were mostly men who did heavy labour, frequently out of doors – butchers, fishmongers and poultry men; pushcart men who sold clothes, fruit, and vegetables; knife-grinders; rag and bone men; sheet-metal workers; carpenters like *Zaida*; plumbers and painters: the panoply of working-class trades from the *shtetls* – ageing immigrants and their first generation sons. They came to Camac to get the fat, grease, gristle and grime out of their skins and the cold out of their bones in winter. The older men spoke Yiddish and English, as did my father, changing from one to the other mid-sentence; the younger men talked in English. Imprecations and curses were almost always in Yiddish. The second generation moved away and Camac closed in the late '80s.

Aaron Wildavsky was a butcher nearly six-and-a-half foot tall with hawser arms, bollard legs and a surprisingly mild disposition. One day after a *platza,* while he and Joe lay near each other wrapped in sheets, Joe got into an argument with him about why Eastern Europe's Jews went so meekly to their deaths. Aaron's mother tongue was Yiddish and he slipped into it more and more often as he tried to counter Joe's contempt. He kept saying, "*Yossel, Yossel, du fa'shtaisht nisht, du fa'shtaisht nisht*",[20] and told him the ruses, reasons and overwhelming force the Nazis used. When Aaron rose to shower and loosed his sheets, I noticed faded black

20. "Joe, Joe, you don't understand, you don't understand."

numbers on his upper left forearm. At the time I thought my father had been cruel; now I think he was scared.

Newsboys hawked the evening dailies between lanes of traffic on the Boulevard when Joe drove home from work or *Schvitz,* and he always tried to time the lights so he could buy a paper. In winter or when it rained, he always bought a paper from them, even if the lights were green.

II

– No Expectations –

Though nothing fixes at conception what we will become, or where we will end – criminal or saint, inner-city shotgun shack or seaside mansion – statistics show that most finish where they start. A boy born in Hell's Kitchen will likely have a harder life, ended in a harder place, than one born the same day on Manhattan's Upper East Side. The smart money in my case was on ending as ex-con rather than saint, on mean streets not East Egg.

That bet looked safe through my high school years. A passage from Rocky Balboa's South Philadelphia to West End London, from inner-city state schools and Catholic commuter college to Cambridge and Yale was unthinkable. John Deans, a reedy, gentle, intellectual boy, had the gym locker above mine in high school; we were not friends. He went to the Ivy League, I to the commuter college. Six years later we met again, on the steps of Yale Law School. I was enrolling, Deans was in his third and final year. "My God! Dan Burt! What are you doing here?"

TODDLER

World War II was ten months old when I was born in Jefferson Hospital, ten blocks from the Store. Two steel trolley tracks trisected the cobbled street outside the Store into nearly equal thirds; trolleys kept them shiny, rolling down them day and night, bells clanging to shove pedestrians and pushcart vendors from their path. The nearest trees were six blocks north, plunked down along the curbs of Spruce and Pine Street; the nearest park, Washington Square, a twenty-minute pram ride northwest.

The Store stood at a refugee crossroads, where the last *shtetl* immigrants traded with black migrants from the Jim Crow South. Its smells, sounds, and faces linger from my infancy. I can still smell dust rising from 60-pound sacks of sawdust hauled from the cellar; woodsmoke and burning fat-tang from fatback piled atop a refrigerated display case; and sickly sweet, moleskin-colour Carnation condensed milk, oozing from a leaky can on a shelf at the dry goods end of the Store, beyond the cold cases. A miasma of squashed pears, bananas, grapes; rotted onions, carrots, apples; dung and piss (horse, dog, cat); smoke from cigarettes and oil drums burning trash to warm the street vendors in winter swirl above the gutters. Mr Segal's corner store reeks of fish. Smells of cumin from rye breads; of garlic and onions from wooden buckets of pickles in brine; of coarse crushed peppercorns coating corned beef and pastrami, puff onto the street from Famous's Delicatessen, an institution then as now, with the creak and slap of its screen door as customers come and go.

The sounds of Yiddish, English, and southern black patois mingled in the streets from 8 a.m. to 6 p.m., business hours. Pushcart vendors – part of the last Jewish wave from the Pale before the 1924 U.S. Immigration Control Act kettled their kinsmen in Eastern Europe – sold fruit, veg, and secondhand clothing to passersby, and spoke Yiddish and its bastard Yinglish among themselves. These *greeners* learnt English sufficiently to trade – "Zo lady, you vant szum apfels?" – adapting traits from their mother-tongue; their hard *g's* and *k's*, softer *ch's* and *sh's*, heard in infancy, left me better able to hear German and Hebrew than French.

Behind plate-glass storefronts across the pavement from the pushcarts, first-generation storekeepers spoke Yiddish to parents, but English to customers, in the flat, nasal *Goodfellas* accent of South Philadalphia, full of reverberant, hard *ng's, o's* turned *uh's* and *er's* turned *ah's*, as in *muthah fuhkah.* "Hello" was a question – *Nu?,*[1] or *Whadda yuh know?* – in Yiddish or English; "goodbye" a hope – *Zei gezint*[2] – or prediction: *See yuh läduh.*

1. "So?"
2. "Go in good health."

The mostly black customers contributed the sibilant, slow drawl of Stephen Foster's darkies to this cacophony. Field hands fleeing the South, drawn by war work in Philadelphia's Navy Yard and factories, crammed the oldest, poorest housing in north and south Philly slums. Their deferential *Yas suh*; *Ah wants dat one*; *be* for *is*, as in *He be cum'n soon*; or *Danny, doan be doin dat* were the only soft sounds on the street. I thought all black people spoke like that until I left Philadelphia for England in 1964; today you have to visit backwoods Mississippi or the red clay hills of Georgia to hear that dialect.

The faces I recall are Mary's, Willy's, and Mr Drucker's. Mary was our *daily,* nearly six-feet tall, a middle-aged, big-breasted *mammy* from the Deep South. She dressed, fed, and pushed me in my stroll-er to Washington Square, or walked behind me as I wobbled up and down Fourth Street. She smiled a lot and called me Danny; there was nothing harsh or frightening in her large face and slow, comforting movements.

We called Willy, Mary's brother, Big Willy. He stood six foot five, and most of a doorway wide, had a hand that could lift a basketball upside-down, and worked beside my father in the butcher shop. He'd driven a Jeep at Anzio for an army officer, seen action, and had the Jeep blown out from under him. Shrapnel buried in his back and shoulders plagued him in winter. Big Willy had the equable temperament of a large man with few natural enemies; only the foolhardy would want to fight someone his size. His face was broad, like his sister's, and he moved with her languid grace; years later, in Saudi Arabia, I worked with a Sudanese lawyer, Abdul Salam al Omari, who looked and moved like him. Willy's curse was alcohol; at least one Monday morning a month he would not appear at 8 a.m. when the store opened, and my father would send Mary to Willy's house, or his girlfriend's, to roust him out.

Our apartment over the Store did not have its own entrance; we had to go up or down a staircase at the back, and then pass through the Store to leave or enter. "Mawnin" or "Aftuhnoon, Lil Joe," Willy would say, when I appeared with Mary for an outing. If there were no customers and he was at a task that could be put by, he would bend down and ask, "Hey, Lil Joe, wunnuh go for a ride?", then swing me seven and a half feet into the air and seat me on his shoulders, walk out through the front door, bending to clear the lintel, and parade up and down the street.

During the day, Mr Drucker's pushcart stood canted forward on its small front wheel like a chicken pecking corn, twenty feet south of the Store. Mr Drucker stood on the curb before it, chanting the day's bargains at passersby. Almost six-foot tall, no more than 160 pounds, his stubble cheeks were sunk, and his gabardine cloth cap, the Jewish push-cart vendor's hallmark summer and winter, greyed and encrusted from weather, car exhaust and fruit-grimed hands. He never failed to hail me, even if he was with a customer. To him I was always *Danila*, never Little Joe, as I was to the black help and customers, or *kleyne Yusselle* (little Joey), as I was to the merchants, like Mr Velushin, whose push-cart was next in line to the south. I never learned where Mr Drucker came from, though most local pushcart men came from the Russian portion of the Pale around Kiev, where my father's family had lived and been murdered. Years later, staring at pictures of Shoah survivors in striped rags before their bunk racks, Mr Drucker rose before me, skeletal rather than gaunt, and I guessed why he might have been so sad and gentle.

My father's face is less distinct than Mary's, Willy's, or Mr Drucker's; he is more of a presence. I don't see him as short, though he was. His hands and feet move fast. He shouts, at Willy, at customers; treads heavily; does not move out of people's way; tears rather than lifts the cellar trapdoor to fetch sacks of rice or stoke the furnace; yanks the front door open when he leaves, slams it behind him; cleaves pork chops from loins like they were Cossack heads. He stares, not looks at people, as if they have done him wrong, or are about to.

I liked it when people called me Little Joe,

though I was not naturally his double. In a picture, aged three, in winter, thick woolen coat, leggings, wool mittens, peaked cap, a toy drum slung from my right shoulder, left thumb near my mouth, though not in it, I stand alone, straight-backed, insolent, indifferent to the camera.

I remember nothing of my mother from toddlerhood; not face, nor voice, nor hands or scent. No incident comes to mind: a void. But if a lover raises her hand to caress me unexpectedly, I flinch.

FRAMEWORK

Parents have favourites. They parcel out attention, instruction, and affection unequally to their children, based on order of birth, sex, looks, a child's strength or weakness or force of personality, and parents' narcissism and aspirations. Isaac favoured Esau, his first born, the hunter. Isaac's wife, Rebecca, doted on Jacob, her second, who lingered in their tents. She prompted and plotted with him to steal Esau's birthright. Cheated, Esau left to form his own tribe, and when Jacob met Esau again, years later, Jacob feared for his life. I was my father's Esau, my brother my mother's Jacob: it is not an uncommon story.

Jungle ethics were our family's touchstone, and I was steeped in them. Along with "Baa, baa black sheep" and "Twinkle, twinkle little star" I was rocked to sleep with

Taffy was a Welshman, Taffy was a thief,
Taffy went to Daddy's store and stole a piece of beef.
Daddy went to Taffy's house, Taffy wasn't home;
Taffy came to Daddy's store and stole a marrow bone.
Daddy went to Taffy's house, Taffy was in bed
Daddy took the marrow bone and bashed in Taffy's head.

Fourth and Bainbridge was not thick with Welshmen, and my parents were notably free of prejudices. Neither was a student of British folklore, and I have no idea where they heard this rhyme, or if one passed it to the other. All its elements appealed: family threat, courage, violence, and effective, vigilante justice. It was their favourite, and it became mine.

I was an undersized, near-sighted child; horses were a blur from a car-length away, until kindergarten, when the defect was discovered and corrected with glasses. I went speechless till past three, learnt to read early, and had a library of superhero, war, and cowboy comics by five. Fears came naturally, fighting was instilled.

From five onwards I feared my father's rage. His ungovernable temper loosed, he struck with belt, fist, brass knuckles, cosh, gaff, pipe, whatever came to hand, until spent. When the Teamsters union, a rough bunch, picketed his store when they were trying to unionize it, I watched him after breakfast prepare to deliver the meat himself, a loaded .38 in a paper bag for the seat beside him, cosh and brass knuckles for jacket pockets, baseball bat for the floor. When he turned into the Mart and made for the picket line, he saw Jack, one of his countermen, walking the picket, and my father tried to run him down.

He beat me with a strap when I was small, for talking back, disobedience, breaking a lamp, staining the carpet, and with his fists when I was older, for intractability, and for hitting my brother. Two beatings stand out. On a hot, sticky, late Sunday summer afternoon in 1948, I was reading a comic on the first-floor landing of our house, three feet from the footstool for his armchair. Half an hour earlier he'd come home from the Store, eaten, and flopped in his chair to smoke a cigarette, read the Sunday papers, and nap. Out of smokes, he commanded, "Danny, go get me a pack of Luckys." I didn't want to stop reading, and his cold command rankled. "No." "What did you say?" "No! Get 'em yourself."

He blew from his chair, dragged me screaming upstairs, and threw me on my bed. "You gonna get me my cigarettes? No? How about now!" And he began to lash my ass with his belt. My mother ran into the bedroom and tried to stop him. She grabbed his arm, but he shook her off. She screamed in English "Joe, Joe, stop it, you'll kill him!", then in the scraps of his mother tongue she knew, "*Yussel, Yussel, Genug! Genug!*"[3] But he flailed away until his rage cooled. Red-rumped and sore, I carried the quarter he forced into my hand to Muchnick's, a corner candy store open till nine, to fetch a pack of Luckys.

The whaling left more than welts; his savagery felt senseless, given the scale of provocation, and it undermined the patriarchal reverence I'd been taught. A few years later, after another beating, all reverence collapsed. He came home, found me hitting my brother, and, without asking why, knocked me four feet across the living room with his first punch.

The childhood fear that endured was want. It was a groundless terror; I never wanted, we were never poor. True, business dwindled with the war's end; as local factories and the Navy Yard cut back, customers moved to where there was more work. From 1946 to 1954 the family spent more than my father earned each year, until his war profits were exhausted and his Store on the brink of failure. But he rented a concession in a farmer's market, and in time did well enough to fish three days a week; he

3. "Enough, enough!"

retired and became a full-time charter captain at sixty.

Yet the fear that we might be homeless or jobless or shamed hung over me like a guillotine, too high to see distinctly, but there, waiting just ahead, honed and ready to sever my neck with a casual pull on the *déclic*. The Depression's hardships crippled my father, and he spoke of them often: wearing his brother's hand-me-downs, leaving school at thirteen to work, selling apples on street corners with his father. He pulsated with worry every day, even when business was good, the ghost of hard times pursuing him even at sea, where, to the last, each day he'd tally the season's fishing trips already sailed, to tell if he was breaking even. I absorbed his dread; glimmering, irrational, marrow-deep.

Tales, hearsay, examples, and training taught me to fight. Dinner times and fishing trips were filled with stories of vengeance, brawling, pride, and violence, my father hero of them all: mauling this or that anti-Semite, telling that cheap boss to "Take this job and shove it!", yanking rude conductors from their trolley cars. All had the same point – "Son, this world is rough / And if a man's gonna make it / He's gotta be tough."[4]

4. "Johnny Cash, "A Boy Named Sue".

I saw him threaten, curse, double men up with a right hook to their guts; watched him short-weight customers; stand unflinching while Holmes, the charter captain who taught him to fish, cut gang-hooks from his cheek when a cast went awry. I watched and cowered when he crashed his fist to the table, he and my mother screaming and cursing each other, throwing plates to the floor.

Boxing lessons complemented the tales. I was four when he first showed me how to make a fist, crouch, raise and bend my right arm to protect my face and belly, while I carried my left just below my left breast, tensed to deliver a haymaker; how to bob, weave, dance out of range, jab, roll with a punch, and shift my weight to put it behind a hook. He would kneel, raise his fists and arms to protect his face and torso, and taunt me to hit him; it was futile. His adult reach, weight and sixteen-inch biceps were impregnable. He flicked each sally off, harder and harder, stinging one side of my face, then the other, with one palm, while he slapped my fist aside with the other, knocking me down, all the while yelling, "C'mon, c'mon! Hit me! Get inside; hit me, hit me", until, frustrated, enraged, and tearful, I charged.

My father repeated these lessons till I was nine or ten. Sometimes I "got inside" the walls of his arms and hit him as hard as I could with my little boy's fists. I would have killed him. But I never learned to box well; small boys, short-sighted and slight, make poor Muhammed Alis. But I did learn to hit first, rush bigger opponents, and pick up whatever came to hand as a weapon if, as usually seemed the case, I was outweighed or outclassed. Rage sank into my cells. When I charged and fought, the true target of fist, club, or writ was my father.

My mother reinforced his teachings. The Gentile boys in our neighbourhood bullied the Jews. A few months after we moved to Whitaker Avenue, a gang of five fixed on me. Their ringleader was Tommy Mann, a half year older and three inches taller than I. I ran into the house whenever I saw him coming, and in time my mother noticed it. When I told her why I'd come in, she told me to go fight him. I whimpered that he was bigger than I, his friends would jump me. Her left hand took my right arm and dragged me down the back steps to the alley, where Tommy and friends loitered; her right hand carried a broom. "Fight him!" She warned his buddies she'd club them with the broom if they interfered, then prodded me towards Tommy with its bristles till we fought.

Several years ago my high school class organized a Fiftieth Reunion. On the back of a form letter encouraging alumni to attend, the organizer wrote a note saying his daughter had married the son of David Gold, a boy I'd played and fought with sixty years before. David asked to be remembered, saying although we often fought he thought we were friends in the end.

He was the local druggist's eldest son, a half-year younger than I. Big for his age, fat, he was a local princeling because his father was a professional and wore a starched, white doctor's tunic while serving malteds at his drugstore soda-fountain. One day when I was nine, David and six of his retainers lined up across the end of our alley and made for my brother, myself, and Warren Sofian, a local boy playing with us. The gang began yelling, tossing garbage as they came; a serious beating loomed. I worried about my brother, seven at the time, too small for the fight ahead. Warren had a large metal cap pistol in a holster at his waist. I grabbed the pistol, grasped it by the barrel so the butt turned billy, and rushed at David. I hit him as hard as I could in the face, above his left eye; he screamed and fell bleeding. It took stitches to close the wound, but the fight was over. I don't recall reasoning that taking out the ringleader would stop the assault, nor thinking what might happen if it didn't.

Our neighbourhood was not a war zone; my father never hit my mother. I played the street ball games of US inner city row-home neighbourhoods, after school and on weekends; played monopoly on rainy days; Saturdays went to the movies to eat popcorn and watch cartoons, until at twelve I began working weekends. We tricked or treated on Halloween, lit firecrackers on the Fourth of July, had newspaper routes, roller-skated down pavement and street, and ice-skated at a rink on the other side of the city. The family ate Chinese on Sunday nights and visited relatives. I read an illustrated Greek myths, and a children's history of western heroes – Davy Crockett at the Alamo, Daniel Boone – till their hard covers crumpled; read *The Reader's Digest* and *Time* in the bathroom and scoured the *Salt Water Sportsman* every month.

Nevertheless, fear and ambition dominated childhood. Suspicion, aggression, violence in home, at school, in the streets, galvanised my small bones, my weak eyes, what intelligence I had, to precipitate my fledgling character. I eyed adults warily as if they might beat me, kids as if they might hurl a rock. Strangers, the slightest challenge, triggered my fight or flight reflex. I developed a volcanic temper and spent years trying to discipline it, questioned authority and often disobeyed it, formed no deep or lasting friendships, and did not trust.

Victories bought my father's favour, weakness my mother's scorn. Hunger for the first, shame from the second, nurtured ambition. "Come you home a hero / Or come not home at all" seeped into my bones long before I read Housman, or heard of Spartan mothers, or watched Tony Soprano's mother, Livia, order him hit. I studied my father's faults to extirpate them in myself, marked the worst beatings for when I might even the score. At thirteen, no one called me Little Joe.

GRADE SCHOOL

Creighton Elementary was an inner city school for the children of truckers, machinists, clerks and a few small tradesmen; the only ones I knew whose parents were professionals were the Gold boys. Perhaps a third of its pupils were Jewish. Almost all of its graduates finished their education at Olney, the local public high school, which they left at eighteen for the army, trades, or minor white collar jobs. The girls got married and were soon pregnant, or the other way round. Two boys out of sixty from my eighth grade class went to Central High, Philadelphia's magnet school for bright boys.

I'd had little experience of other children when we moved to North Philadelphia in 1947 and, a few months later, entered kindergarten. I was reading by then and paid no attention to threshold alphabet or reading lessons. Next year, in first grade, my printing slanted the wrong way because I was left-handed. The rote-learning arithmetic bored me; no one could explain why 1 + 1 must equal 2, and I had trouble with it. Games were problematic; no one wanted on his team a diminutive batter who wore Coke-bottle glasses, and I disliked team sports. When boys yelled, "Hey, four-eyes!" I'd hit them, which made me a discipline problem.

The first grade teacher, Mrs Grey, was a kindly woman who helped me through the year. Her second grade successor, Miss Fitzmaurice, was a hatchet-faced, fifty-year-old Calvinist in tweed suits and starched white blouses with a reputation for breaking mavericks. She favoured brimstone hued suitings, wore thin silver glasses that hung a few inches above her modest breasts from a gold-link chain, or perched like a *pince-nez* on her nose, and had a screeching voice, the sound of rat claws scratching glass.

I could not please Miss Fitzmaurice: my sums were wrong, my times tables faulty, and I never knew where we were when the class read *Dick and Jane*. Worst of all, I tried to use my left hand to write when she began to teach us script. My *p*'s and *q*'s slanted left, when she insisted that they lean right; hung on the wall for parents' day they boldly ran *à rebours*, and Miss Fitzmaurice was not having a little Huysmans in her second grade. Seven years old, in 1949, I met my Nemesis.

She broadcast my mistakes to the class, gave me extra homework, kept me in at recess, stood me for a half hour in the cloak room for inattention or arithmetic errors, and, worst of all, for writing with my left hand; she branded me intractable and sent me to the principal for discipline. I tried to satisfy her and cried over my homework regularly. Report card days twice a semester inscribed my shame; columns of blue *U*'s (for "unsatisfactory") opposite "arithmetic", "reading", "penmanship", "gym", "drawing", "neatness", "cooperation" – all leaning in the right direction in Miss Fitzmaurice's flawless hand – filled the piece of folded cardboard I reluctantly carried home. My parents did not question her judgement on parents' night when they came to discuss my performance.

My right hand was shaping cursive script slanted right rather than left by the time the school year ended, but it looked more like a Twombly charcoal than a legible hand. Miss Fitzmaurice pinned a note to my sweater to take home several weeks before our last report card was due. It said I would not be promoted to the third grade with the rest of the second graders, was to be sent to a special school for slow learners, and would have to repeat second grade. This my parents could not accept.

A few mornings later, instead of the yellow bus to school, I boarded the "R" bus to Frankfurt with my mother, then the El, a train that ran on elevated tracks for several miles before descending under center city Philadelphia. We climbed the steps from the subway at Broad and Walnut and walked several blocks down Walnut Street to an imposing, five-story brownstone divided into apartments, with eight doorbells beside brass plaques. We waited in one of the apartments until a gentleman in his fifties – gold-rimmed glasses, waistcoat with gold fob-chain slung across, thinning hair, avuncular demeanor – opened a frosted glass-panel door from an inner room, walked over to us, and surprised me by smiling, asking my name, telling me his, and putting me at ease. He asked my mother if she would mind waiting while he and I went into his office to play some games. We entered his office and he closed the door. I was in a large room, desk piled with papers, book-lined walls, and leather couch near a low table with three child-sized chairs around it. We talked awhile, I told him about school, what I loved and loathed; then we played some games and I solved some puzzles he gave me.

My mother, twisted handkerchief in hand, rose when I emerged; she left me rifling through pictures in old copies of *Life* while she went into the inner room. Twenty minutes or so later she came out, tearful, an envelope in hand, and we left to board the subway home. She walked me to school next day, met with the principal and Miss Fitzmaurice, and gave them the letter. Creighton promoted me to the third grade with the rest of my class. Years later I learned that he was a child psychologist, our games were IQ tests, and he did not think I was retarded. If there is a hell, I will surely go there, but skippingly, so long as Miss Fitzmaurice is there too, in the eighth circle, along with Caiaphas and other Pharisees.

School dread diminished after I left Miss Fitzmaurice's class. But, while there were fewer *U*'s, when the baby-boomer flood swamped state schools four years later, and they coped by ordering the best students to *skip* a half year, I was not chosen.

I have only three Creighton memories from the subsequent six years there: learning to make zip guns in Shop; suspension for emulating characters in *Blackboard Jungle*; and Charlene Cores. The curriculum included mandatory vocational classes for both sexes in grades seven and eight, our last two years before high school. Girls went to Home Ec and learned to sew, bake, and clean; boys to Shop, where they used handsaws, hammers, and screwdrivers to waste white pine and shellac making footstools, book racks and pencil trays. Our one memorable product was extracurricular.

A few classmates were older, confirmed delinquents, who had done time in reform schools. One day in eighth grade Shop one of these boys taught us to make a zip gun. You draw a butt with, say, a six-inch barrel on a length of 2x4, cut the shape out, then fashion it into the semblance of a wooden gun with coping saw, file and sandpaper. Next, rout a channel half an inch deep the length of the barrel, place a six-inch length of copper tubing in it and tape the tube tightly to the barrel with duct tape. A small screw is sharpened, punched through a thick rubber band, the band stretched across the end of the tube and nailed to the butt for a firing pin; so when the screw is stretched and released, its sharp end slams a sixteenth of an inch into the tube.

You're in business: place a .22 calibre shell in the butt-end of the tube, draw the rubber band and hope for the best. Zip guns were often more dangerous to the user than the target, the round exploding in the tube and spraying its user with copper shrapnel. But at close range, five to ten feet, and if all went well, a zip gun could kill. Teenagers used them in gang fights in the 1950s, when guns were less ubiquitous than they are now, and drug trafficking hadn't enriched gang members; prisoners still use them.

Rebellion is a hallmark of puberty, and puberty struck hard at twelve. One weekday in late spring, 1955, Irv Cossrow and I cut school and went to see a new movie, *Blackboard Jungle*. Sociologists mark the film's release as the start of the American youth revolt that peaked in the 1960s. Its theme music, Bill Haley's "Rock Around the Clock", became our teen anthem. We imagined ourselves *Blackboard Jungle's* bored, dangerous, juvenile delinquents in an inner-city school, good at heart, and unfairly charged with threatening our teacher. We, not Sidney Poitier, charged the villain with the pointy end of a flagpole; we could be cool like Vic Morrow. The movie caused riots in some cities, and the Eisenhower administration refused to approve it as the US entry at Cannes. Irv and I pushed out through the movie house's glass doors that afternoon, blinking in the sunlight and singing "One, two, three o'clock, four o'clock rock / Five, six, seven . . . / We're gonna rock, around, the clock tonight . . ." as loud as we could: we were transfigured.

A year before this metamorphosis the Cossrows had come to our neighborhood from the Bronx. Irv's father, Nate, a failed Manhattan furrier, bought the corner grocery store across the street from our house. He and his wife, Gertrude, whom we named Dirty Girty, kept store from 7 a.m. to 7 p.m.; in ten years it failed too. Nate was thin, worn, avuncular. Gertrude, a half-foot taller, fifty pounds heavier, a cigarette dangling from her lower lip, its ash threatening to thicken the pans of coleslaw or barrels of pickles, did the heavy lifting in the shop. You could imagine Dirty Girty repairing Russian tanks at Stalingrad, immovable under a Nazi barrage.

Suki, Irv's older sister by five years, was thin but big-breasted, medium height, with high cheekbones, long blonde hair which never seemed clean, pale, northern Russian skin like all the Cossrows, and full lips. She aped Brigitte Bardot and was the subject of much salacious speculation.

It's difficult for a newcomer to fit into a neighbourhood at twelve, Irv's age when the family moved to Philadelphia. Twelve and thirteen-year olds are naturally clannish, their customs and rituals mysterious to an interloper, who is particularly vulnerable to exclusion if he or his family looks and behaves differently from the locals. Irv was preternaturally tall and gangling, nearly six feet; more sophisticated than us, having grown up in the Bronx; had parents we mocked, especially his mother; and generally thought, or pretended to think of himself as a superior being. Nature and chance seemed stacked against him; he committed suicide before he was thirty.

Irv and I, outsiders both, were friends for a few years; high schools parted us, and that metamorphic movie afternoon was friendship's high point. We decided to buy black motorcycle boots, jeans, turtlenecks and leather jackets, and wear this gangster garb to school to announce our coming of age. Irv suggested we cap our outfits with black berets and call ourselves The Black Pierres. The suggestion must have been his, because at the time I might have been able to find France on a globe, but no more. Next day we marched into our seventh grade classroom, proclaimed our new identities to teacher and classmates, and were suspended minutes later.

My parents did not harangue or punish me for this suspension, nor those that punctuated my high school years. They had no concern for education as a process or end in itself; only for its possible social and commercial consequences. My mother coveted the prestige that would accrue from having a college graduate son but counted on my brother to provide it. He did not disappoint her. When Creighton "skipped" the five brightest children in grades five, six, and seven to relieve over-crowding, he was one of his grade's five.

My father's fundamental values trumped the lip-service he paid to education. For him, education's purpose was to make money. He told me often I should "Get an education, 'cause they can't take that from you", but did nothing to encourage my studies. I had little will to swot up lessons after working thirty-odd hours, Thursdays through Sundays, in his butcher shop. He had little regard for teachers and none for intellectuals. He respected charter captains, like Holmes, and boxers; he was proud I broke rules and got into trouble – it was what real boys did. If that meant poor school performance, so be it. There was more than a tinge of the sociopath in Joe.

BUTCHER SHOPS

Butcher shops, Central High, the sea and girls schooled late childhood and adolescence, school as such the least important.

The Store

Mort Tannenbaum, a tall, porky, buttoned-up, grey-suited man, carrying a large black briefcase, made weekly house calls on small businessmen like my father, whose accountant he was. Monday nights at 7 p.m. they sat side by side at the dining-room table, so close their knees touched, examining black columns on pale blue-lined graph paper that autopsied the Store's prior week's performance, often totaled in red ink at the bottom right. He was a meek angel of death.

Joe would call Louise to the dining room after Mort's visitations and show her the papers he had left. Her face would fall, then their voices; they'd talk of cutting expenses or another trip to the safe deposit box for the residue of the war profits. Then Joe binned the papers. He continued to fish once a week at least; Louise missed no beauty appointments and kept her "daily" on; but I understood the Store was in trouble and my duty was to help.

Old enough for a paper route, I began delivering the *Evening Bulletin* after school and on weekends.

And, from the spring of 1952, my father shanghaied me on Sundays to wash platters, sweep, and do odd jobs if his regular cleaning man was absent. He paid me $.25 an hour and my mother did not object. I was nine and a half.

We left at 7.30 a.m. in his brown, 1947, ex-Phillip Morris delivery van. It had no passenger seat; I sat in the middle of the spare tire on the floor boards where the passenger seat should have been and held on to the door frame to keep from sliding as we bounced over cobbles and slewed in trolley tracks down Fifth Street towards the Store. Big Willey dressed me in a clean apron and butcher's coat, hems hiked and cuffs rolled to fit my four-foot frame, and by 8.30 a.m., more swaddled than clothed, I was washing platters.

The wash tub was a fifty-gallon stainless-steel can set over a drain below a spigot in the right-hand corner of the tiny cutting room at the rear of the Store. Beside the tub were two chopping blocks, stacked with dozens of yard-long, greasy, blood-congealed platters, weighing fifteen to twenty pounds, their enamel chipped from years of use. Opposite, by the back door, clumps of soiled *greens* soaked in two ten-gallon tin buckets that had once held chitterlings. *Greens* were platter-length, grooved steel rods, holding three-inch tall, bunched green rubber strips no thicker than a matchbook; they were inserted between platters to suggest freshness.

I stood on an upturned Coke case beside the tub, filled two-thirds full with the hottest water I could bear, immersed six or seven platters, one at a time, added two cups of strong soap powder, a half-glass of ammonia, and washed: scrub the platter's top half with a stiff bristle brush, turn it end for end, wash the bottom half, then balance it on the tub rim below the spigot and rinse. The last *greens* and platters lay drying on the block just before lunch.

After lunch I raked the cellar floor, shovelled spilled rice, beans, burst cans, and rat shit into a garbage can, and sprinkled fresh sawdust, terrified a rat would jump me from behind a sack or carton. Then I swept and sprinkled the Store's floor, restocked the bags below the back counter, and, with the help of a stepladder, the dry-goods shelves in front, and washed the outside of the display-case windows with ammonia and clean rag.

Done most Sundays before closing time, I stood behind the counter watching my father wait trade, bag orders, and make change. Some of the women, as well as the men, were hung over or still drunk after Saturday night. Joe's thumb, hidden below the counter-top, held down the paper under the meat he was weighing; his pencil paused as he added a column of prices incorrectly in his favour, bantering with the customers while he robbed them. Sometimes he had me carry a large bag around the counter to a customer, rather than lifting it over the countertop to them himself, while he made change for a ten, rather than the twenty he'd been given. They'd say, "Thank yuh, L'll Joe." Some tipped me a nickel or dime, and I would drop my head, red-faced, mute, avoiding their eyes; they thought me shy.

Pennsauken

Childhood's venues changed at twelve and a half, when I went to work in the Pennsauken Merchandise Mart, a windowless "farmers' market" on forty level acres in New Jersey, five minutes across the Delaware River from Philadelphia. Joe bought a half interest in a butcher shop there after he closed his failing Fourth Street store.[5] To save money he put me to work in the cutting room and on the counter selling lunchmeat. The partnership ruptured within two years, leaving my father in possession.

The Mart was a one-storey, flat-roofed yellow cinderblock coffin, floating in an open sea of asphalt where a thousand cars could park. Five blocks long, two boxcars wide, it took more than ten minutes to walk one of its two aisles end to end. Customers,

5. See page 14.

almost all of whom were working class or poor, entered through eight steel double doors evenly spaced down its two long sides, or the double glass doors at either end. It had no windows or skylights; once inside, whether it was night or day, fair or foul became a mystery, except when hail or heavy rain thrummed on the sheet-metal roof. You could see heat rise in waves from the asphalt parking lot, the Mart shimmer when the temperature hit one hundred degrees in summer, and feel the tar suck your shoes down as you walked across the melting parking lot. But you could not see, or smell, or hear childhood any longer.

The Pennsauken Merchandise Mart circa 1954
(arrow marks Pennsauken Meats)

The Mart's two uncarpeted concrete aisles, each a car-length wide, were stained with grime from patrons' work boots and plimsolls. There was neither air-conditioning nor insulation. Six-foot-long fluorescent lights, two to a pod, hung ten feet from the floor, ran almost unbroken down both sides of the

Mart's two aisles, tinting trade and tradesmen slightly green. A P.A. system blared country music (Hank Williams, Gentleman Jim Reeves, Patsy Cline, and Ernest Tubbs), Fifties rock (Elvis, the Shirelles, Chuck Berry) and Pop (Peggy Lee's "How Much Is That Doggy In The Window", Pat Boone singing "Love Letters in the Sand"), from opening till closing time, except at Christmas, when Alvin and The Chipmunks squeaked "Here Comes Santa Claus", "We Wish You a Merry Christmas", "Rudolph the Red Nosed Reindeer"; Bing Crosby crooned "White Christmas", and various groups and solos wailed the traditional religious songs ("Silent Night", "God Rest Ye, Merry Gentlemen", "Away in a Manger") in an infinite loop.

Along the grey aisles, stalls crowded with folding tables were piled with boxes of seconds: Levis, Keds, socks, underpants, panties, bras, sweaters, skirts, wash'n'wear white shirts, clip-on ties, and caps. Lunch counters sold Philly steak sandwiches, hot dogs, burgers, french fries, kielbasa on buns, Coke, caffeinated coffee, ice cream, snow cones;[6] sweets-stands vended soft pretzels, popcorn plain and candied, cotton candy, candy apples, jaw breakers, Hershey bars, chocolate kisses, candy of every description. Other stalls offered axes, Bowie knives, shot guns, rifles, hunting bows, work boots, foul-

6. Crushed ice with soda syrup poured over it.

weather gear; reject bowls, plates, cutlery, pots and pans; light fishing tackle, toys, bicycles, strollers, belts, coats, tropical fish, pets, and pet supplies; the staples of the working poor.

Wednesday nights at 6 p.m. the Mart awoke to chains rattling up through eye-bolts. Merchants opened locks, raised chain-link shutters, and bedded down at ten to their jangling descants. Open forty-two of the next ninety-six hours, twelve hours Friday, fourteen hours Saturdays, it accommodated the rhythm of the working man's week; not a destination shopping center, it attracted no rubberneckers.

I worked there fifty weeks a year for the next eight years. Friday 4 p.m. to midnight and Saturdays 8 a.m. to 6 p.m. stretched to Thursday nights through Sundays by the time I was sixteen, with the exception of one three-month interlude. My last working day at Pennsauken was the Sunday before Christmas, 1963.

The three-month hiatus occurred a year into my hitch, coinciding with the hiring of a new cashier. She was the only woman employee; fetching, mid-thirties, long black colleen hair, blue eyes, long thin legs, she lightened the atmosphere in the place. My father began to take pains with his appearance, curse less, take longer lunch breaks. A few weeks after she entered the cashier's booth, my presence seemed less essential; I was given occasional Friday nights off and sent home early some Saturdays. Longer hours resumed when Uncle Al, my mother's detective brother, produced proof of dalliance and the cashier was fired.

Pennsauken Meats had two parts, the back room – hidden from customers, where meat and poultry were received, prepared and stored – and the counter, a line of white enamelled refrigerated cases, where this meat and poultry were displayed and sold. The back room was the store's industrial heart, a windowless, eighteen-by-thirty foot rectangle with three walk-in ice boxes, chopping blocks, cutting table, slicers, grinder, band-saw and wash tubs. Knives, cleavers, slicers and saw blades were all that gleamed there. An automatic slicer the size of a V8 car engine; a meat grinder with throat as large as a man's forearm; a Hobart band-saw, six feet tall with a 110″ circular blade, a ½″ wide and three teeth to the inch – these growled, screamed and whirred all day long. The back room sounded like a machine shop.

You could hear rats – we called them freezer rats – scuttle away when you opened the door to the large walk-in freezer opposite the back room. They gnawed through a foot of concrete foundation and three-inch plywood floor to nibble frozen turkeys stored for the holidays. We shaved the chewed areas with the band-saw to remove the teeth marks before the turkeys went on sale. When we made sausage, you could smell the rancid grease from the green pork trimmings that comprised it, as well as the sage mixed with sodium nitrite to turn the trimmings pink again.

Frankie, the deli man, sliced lunchmeats, helped make hamburger and sausage, cut up frying chickens for sale as breasts, legs, wings and giblets, and generally cleaned; I was his understudy. Lean, five-nine, black, about twenty-five, he developed his heavily muscled body in the prison where he spent two years before coming to work at Pennsauken. He straightened and pomaded his hair, wore a *do-rag*[7] after the fashion of gang members, was a professional-level checkers and ping pong player – also courtesy of the Penitentiary – and a rough trade's gentle teacher.

We sold nearly a third of a ton of sliced lunchmeats between 5 p.m. Friday night and 11 p.m. Saturday, all of it sliced by Frankie and me. He showed me how to set the slicer's blade for slice thickness. Each item had its setting: cut too fine, the meat or cheese broke up; too thick and it made poor sandwiches; either way it wouldn't sell. Frankie taught me to slice faster by darting my hand under the slicer's stacking arm on its upswing and whisking a

7. Pronounced *doo* as in *hair-do*.

lunchmeat pile from the slicer tray while the slicer ran, so it didn't stop till a whole baloney or ham was sliced. The slicer ran from 8 a.m. till 10 p.m. Fridays, Saturdays 8 a.m. to 8 p.m. Clean, set, slice, platter, store in the deli box; clean, set, slice . . . over and over, twelve hours a day.

I learned to push hamburger and sausage while standing on a rickety stool above the grinder tray, feeding scraps into its maw so they emerged smoothly from the forcing plate into the hands of the butcher below me. Frankie taught me to cut and platter the frying chickens that came buried in congealed ice inside flimsy, thin-slatted pine crates, each weighing north of sixty pounds, bound with stapled hanger-wire. Grasp a chicken's legs, drag it from the ice, sever legs, wings, and back from breast, nick breast-bone so the breast spreads easily, then pile the parts separately for plattering. Within weeks it took no more than ninety seconds from the time I plunged my hand into the ice until the severed parts joined their proper piles.

Chickens are dirty birds, their frozen tombs no cleaner. The ice's jagged edges pricked fingers and wrist as you jammed your hand in to extract a chicken; the fowls' sharp shank spurs jabbed your palm as you tightened your grip to pull them out. No one wore gloves, none was offered. I was slicing lunchmeats one Saturday a few hours after segmenting fryers when a lump began to form in my armpit and my temperature began to rise. I told one of the butchers cutting pork chops at his block across the room, and he came over, took my arm, turned it palm up and pointed to a red line running up the vein from my wrist to armpit: blood poisoning. Frankie drove me in the truck to the emergency room, where I gave my name, age (thirteen and a half) and address, received a shot, and went back to work. The tell-tale line, the swelling and fever reappeared a few months later, again a few hours after cutting up chickens. I took a taxi to the hospital, asked the driver to wait, and returned to work after the injection. This process repeated itself once or twice each year while I worked at Pennsauken. Gloves would have reduced the risk but slowed the dismembering. It was faster and cheaper to risk occasional septicaemia and a quick visit to hospital than take seconds more per chicken.

When we were busiest, breaks were few and short; piss outside against the wall between the back room door and walk-in freezer; fifteen minutes for hamburger, fries, and coffee at the lunch counter next door; perhaps thirty-minutes break in a twelve-hour Saturday. I was wolfing a burger at the lunch counter one Saturday just before noon, some months into my apprenticeship, in gory apron and butcher's coat. A prim, school-marmish, older woman stopped for a coffee, noticed me, and asked, "How old are you, young man?" "Thirteen."

"Do you work at that butcher's next door?" "Yes, ma'am." "You shouldn't be working there!" She downed her coffee, stepped up to our meat counter and asked for the manager. I heard her tell my father it was illegal to employ a boy my age in a butcher shop, and that she was going to report him. If she did, no one did anything about it.[8]

Pennsauken's counter – ten cases, each four-foot high and three-foot wide, packed with sixteen kinds of thinly sliced deli, cuts of beef, veal and pork, chickens, turkeys, hamburger and sausage – ran the length of two buses down the Mart's north aisle. I was taught to work it a few months after starting in the back room: how to stand, greet shoppers, weigh, bag, make change, and read a scale. Each cut's price per pound fronted every platter in the case, but when the counterman weighed an item, the scale showed the customer only the weight, though the counterman could see weight and cost in the magnifying window on his side of the scale. The customer knew the correct cost of what was weighed only if 1) the weight equalled the per-pound posted price, 2) you told her, or 3) she could multiply and divide fractions handily. Few could.

8. Federal and state laws have long prohibited persons under eighteen from working in hazardous places and deem a cutting room a hazardous place. Cf. 29 CFR secs. 570.2(a)(2); 570.6.

My father taught me to steal after I learned to read scales. He told me we advertised lower prices than the chain stores to compete, and, at those prices, we might well lose money or, at best, break even. To make a profit we had to add five percent to every sale. Then he showed me how.

We eschewed the crude methods he'd used in the Store: holding down scale-paper, sliding boxes of lard onto weighing pans, short-changing. At Pennsauken Meats we cheated customers by exploiting their difficulty with fractions. The trick was to avoid even weight. Boiled ham was $.89 a pound, i.e. 5½ cents an ounce; if asked for a pound, you laid enough on the scale so that, even after removing a few slices, more than a pound remained. "A little over OK?", and if so, you charged for a pound and three ounces ($1.05 with rounding), not the pound and two ounces ($.99) the scale showed.

Were odd weight opportunities lacking, you estimated the bill as you began toting, calculated five percent, and added that amount to the total. Sometimes you used both methods. If caught using either, you apologized, corrected the bill, and fixed the customer's face in mind, in case she shopped there again. Most walked away unaware they'd been cheated.

Every week I stole, from every customer I could steal from, and mostly got away with it. Few expected a boy to fleece them. I chattered so as to ingratiate and distract; studied clothes, faces, conversations to guess those brighter or more alert and harder to cheat. A fair few became regulars and trusted me. From them I stole ten percent, to keep my average up. Almost all were working-class women in shabby clothes, thin coats in winter, with poor teeth, squalling infants or puling toddlers, faces smeared with chocolate or lollipops, tugging their mothers' skirts.

I flushed with shame, not embarrassment, whenever I was caught, once or twice a week, making hard lots harder. I was ashamed each time I cheated, and I waited on tens of thousands in those eight years on the counter. The sense of guilt stayed with me. Ever since, when an affair begins, I rehearse the five percents with my new lover.

CENTRAL HIGH

Central High School sits like the Acropolis on a hill at Ogontz and Olney Avenues, in the Logan section of North Philadelphia. For 175 years superior secondary schoolers city wide have gone there to prepare for the colleges they will nearly all attend; it offers no vocational courses, no carpentry or plumbing, no bricklaying; famous alumni are legion: Thomas Eakins, Daniel and Simon Guggenheim, Alexander Woolcott, Louis Kahn, Albert Barnes, Noam Chomsky, Bill Cosby, and more; and alone among

U.S. public high schools it may confer an academic degree, the BA. But I knew none of this in 1956. Olney was my neighbourhood high school, which almost all Creightonians attended. Olney graduates were unlikely to go to college, and Olney was where I was headed, until puppy love took a hand.

We call lust love at thirteen. Charlene Cores – a slight, blue-eyed, black-haired girl – lived four long blocks away across Roosevelt Boulevard, the eight-lane highway bisecting our neighbourhood. She was probably in my class from first grade, but I didn't notice her till puberty sharpened my sight. Charlene, however, would have been happy had I remained blind: Valentine's, Christmas cards, home runs smashed in half-ball as she passed by, devotion confessed to her friends had no more effect on her than did moping past her house at night or dating her best friend, Sonia Steinberg, to induce jealousy. But perhaps she would admire me if I went to Central, and admiration morph to more?

All I knew about Central was it did not take all-comers. You had to apply: boys with higher IQ scores had a right to enroll, those with lower scores had to pass an entrance exam. I had done well in the ubiquitous mid-Fifties American IQ tests; perhaps I wouldn't have to take the exam and likely fail. No grade school teacher said "Try Central"; my parents objected, "too far away, you're no student, nobody you know's going". Charlene failed to swoon when told that Central might have me; but I persevered, too young to understand that pheromones remain indifferent to test scores and determination.

I climbed the hill towards Central's three embossed, twelve-feet-high, steel-fronted doors the Thursday after Labor Day, 7 September 1956. Charlene went to Olney. Central did not impress her, nor I it: an hour after my first day there began, I shuffled back home down the hill, suspended within minutes of arriving. Charlene never spoke to me again, not even at our grade school class reunion in 1986, when she ignored me as she had thirty years before.

Behind Central's front doors the main hall ran the length of half a football field to the South Lawn, where at lunch break in good weather we dawdled, snuck cigarettes, and occasionally fought. That first day, the hall's sixteen-foot ceilings and marble walls bearing portraits of past school presidents and notable alumni cowed me. Signs labeled Orientation and older boys with armbands herded us up four flights to the top-floor lunch room, which served 400 at a time; it could have been an army mess hall. Rows of yard-wide, three-inch-thick, rectangular oak-top dining tables, drawn up in serried ranks like soldiers on parade, flanked the stainless-steel serving counters. Each table sat forty boys, twenty a side, on round oak stool tops bolted to curved steel arms, hinged to the table's central support; diners swung the seats out to sit, and back when they rose. We found a table posted with the first letter of our last name, sat, and waited for Orientation to begin.

Most of the boys knew what to expect. They lived in middle- and upper-middle-class homes, 80 percent of them Jewish, in Oak Lane, Oxford Circle, Mount Airy, Wynnefield and Society Hill – Philadelphia's better parts. Second-generation Central boys whose fathers had gone to college were not unusual. They came in cliques from gleaming junior high schools, where they had spent grades six, seven, and eight preparing for Central, with a view to college. They were ambitious, superior, self-confident, elitist, and they disdained outsiders.

Elmer Field, Central's president ("principal" in lesser schools) called, "Boys, Boys," welcomed us to ninth grade, and began explaining how to find our home rooms, where each morning we would meet before class for roll-taking and administrative matters. I turned to the boy on my left and asked, "What's a Home Room?" Two seats to my right across the table, a boy guffawed: "Hey, look at that shmuck; he doesn't even know what a Home Room is!" I flushed, sprang across the table, and knocked him off his stool. We were quickly parted, and I was sent, not for the last time, to Mr Christman, vice-principal and disciplinarian, who suspended me.

My parents didn't punish me. My father would

have done the same, and he was quietly proud. My mother's clan would have done worse. And, my parents no longer had a lash to hand: I was too big to beat (I might hit back), had little free time to dock (school, homework, and butcher shop took almost all of it), no allowance to halt (I earned my spending money); and my father wouldn't forfeit cheap, trusted labour that allowed him to fish a second or third day each week.

Central forbade us to *break bounds* – leave school grounds – for lunch; we had to buy it in the cafeteria or "brown-bag" it from home. But school food was execrable, brown-bagging a nuisance and "square". There were hamburgers and hot dogs, Cokes and malteds at the luncheonettes a short sprint past the school monitors up Olney Avenue, where our lit cigarettes smoldered on the steel rims of pinball machines pinging and flashing away, and fumes from the grease and oil in which your order fried made your mouth water. Mr Christman suspended me a third time that year, not for fighting, or cutting class, but for breaking bounds. He insisted this time that my father, rather than my mother, come to school to reinstate me.

We filed into his office for our audience: swarthy, thick-armed ghetto butcher; fair skinned, white-gloved housewife, fattened from a third child in her late fertile years; pint-sized, slouching ninth grader. John D. Christman unfolded himself from behind his desk to receive us, a dark grey three-piece suit, gold watch fob with what might have been a dangling Phi Beta Kappa key slung across his undistended stomach, thin white hair combed straight back and trimmed short of a white collar – six inches taller than my five-foot-five father, and every inch a WASP. We sat before him in a row while he chastised me.

He rehashed the rule against breaking bounds and reminded me this was not the first time I'd been caught. He explained the rule's reasons and intoned the consequences for flaunting it. "Now, give me your word you won't leave school grounds again during lunch period." "No! School food stinks." He turned to my father, "You see, Mr Burt, what we're up against . . ." and waited for his reply. "Well, how bad is the school food?" I suffered more suspensions during my Central years, but my father was not requested to attend another reinstatement.

Classwork was no more palatable than school lunches. We studied set subjects in the ninth grade – English, Algebra, Latin, History, Science, Social Studies, and Art – and were graded twice a year, at the end of each semester. If you failed Latin 1A in the fall semester, you had to repeat and pass it in the spring, then take Latin 1B at summer school to stay with your class. You could end up attending school twelve months a year during your four high-school years, if you failed consistently, and in my first two years that's what I did, flunking two subjects the first year, one the second. But with electives, one teacher's interest and a second unrequited love, came better grades; the last two years I avoided summer school.

John Mulloy taught European history at Central during the day, and at La Salle College, a Christian Brothers institution, three nights a week. He was a first- or, at most, second-generation Irish American, five foot ten or so, with tortoise-shell oval glasses above crooked yellow teeth, purple-pocked face – so gaunt he might have landed from Famine Galway. Catholicism enveloped and sustained him; he had six children, an ash cross on his forehead every Wednesday at the start of Lent, and he regarded Chartres, Aquinas and monasticism as the consummation of European history. Mr Mulloy, humble before his God, was a counter-cultural figure amidst Central's striving Jewish majority.

Average sophomores at Central chose one elective in tenth grade; members of the advanced class, the top ten percent, could choose two. Modern European History interested my father; he followed international news in the local press and on national radio and TV; read historical novels from the *Reader's Digest Condensed Book Club*; articles on foreign affairs and history in *Reader's Digest, Life* and *Time*. He argued about pre-war Europe with immigrant acquaintances at *Schvitz* and with his sons, when they began to learn about such things in their grade school *Weekly Readers*. I chose Modern European History as my tenth grade elective, in a class of mostly advanced students who had chosen it as their second.

The boys besieged Mr Mulloy from the outset, and he was often outmatched. He knew more, of course, but they were smarter, with quicker minds. Virtues he claimed for what they believed were "the dark ages" were inconsistent with what they'd been taught; and medieval achievements of a culture that brought their forebears pogroms, and, at its end, the Inquisition, were always going to be a hard sell. Many in the class were headed for careers in science, medicine or law. Their rationalist faith held revealed religion in teenage contempt. A few were bullies.

Michael Kirsch, their ringleader, for example: fifteen, in the advanced class, Mulloy's height, sporting vestigial baby fat, smart clothes, popularity. He wore the black wool bomber jacket of a Jewish Greek-letter fraternity to class each day: gold-piped sleeves, cuffs, waist band, gold collar, gold *AZA* in Roman letters across its front, "Mike" in cursive on the back. From his second-row seat by the windows, opposite the door, Mike Kirsch raised his hand in Mr Mulloy's face every day to argue and quibble for his peers' amusement, waste time, and try the patience of John Mulloy. No one took the teacher's side.

I sat in the back, silent, ignored, where the rear and door-side walls met, ten rows diagonally behind and to the right of Kirsch. Modern European History intrigued me: my paternal grandmother, still hale and vicious, had lived part of it; I knew men who'd been in the camps. Like me, Mulloy was a Central outsider, though for different reasons. His Catholic, spiritual critique of American materialism and exceptionalism sounded in me. I wanted to hear what he had to say; I wanted Kirsch to shut up.

Had I hit Kirsch in class I would have been expelled, rather than suspended, and by the end of class the fury always passed. Some three weeks into term, seething with frustration, I spoke up on Mulloy's side during an inane argument and, to my surprise, silenced Kirsch. As I left class, Mulloy told me to come to his office during lunch period. There, he praised my argument, and me for speaking up, asked where I lived, what school I'd come from, and invited me to drop by again to talk. I was suspicious – no teacher had shown interest in me before. But if the Temple veil was not rent that lunchtime, there was at least a small tear.

III

– The Blue Guitars –

The man replied, 'Things as they are
Are changed upon the blue guitar'

– Wallace Stevens, "The Man with the Blue Guitar"

JOHN MULLOY

Mr Mulloy's refuge was on Central's second floor, above the doors to the South Lawn: a narrow rectangle, three doorways wide, squeezed by books shelved floor to ceiling down east and west walls. A standard-issue, yellowed oak office desk stood before the south window at the far end. Two chairs faced the desk, and behind the desk sat Mr Mulloy, back to the window, facing the door five yards away. It was a good defensive position.

His invitation offered an alternative to disruption, cutting class, and mooching about with hunched shoulders looking for an excuse to fight. But what would we talk about? I paid more attention in his class, read the textbook, and thought about both. If a question went unanswered or unasked in class, I'd stop by to talk about it. By academic year's end we were talking in his office half an hour each week.

Words worked no miracles; I failed another course that year and went to summer school again, but for one subject, not two. After our conversations began, I still fought, cut classes and school, but less. We talked more the next year, when he did not teach me, and often twice a week in my senior year. History and politics were not our only subjects. I told him about Pennsauken, girls, drag-racing, and what had grown to my loathing for classmates and their superciliousness. He listened, countered Madison Avenue and "Engine Charlie" Wilson[1] with Maritain and Huizinga, Levittown with Notre Dame.

John F. Kennedy began his run for the Democratic presidential nomination in New Hampshire in January, 1960, the beginning of my last term at Central. The country wondered whether a Catholic could be elected president in Protestant America. Mr Mulloy recalled Catholic Al Smith's loss to Hoover in 1928 and wondered had the country changed. For the first time I saw bigotry's scars on a man not black or Jewish. When JFK won the primary in West Virginia, a southern Baptist stronghold, Mulloy walked taller into his classes.

1. Charles Erwin Wilson, known as Engine Charlie, CEO of GM and Eisenhower's Secretary of Defense, was famous for having said during a Congressional hearing that "What was good for . . . America was good for GM, and vice versa".

Life magazine ran a feature on Kennedy's Hyannis and Harvard – photos of grey shingle "cottages" on Cape Cod beaches, sail boats, blue blazers and white ducks, grand-columned Widener library, red-and-gold leaved "Yard", and red-brick student dorms called "Houses", named for the Brahmin dead. My mentor told me what little he knew about this Olympus that he had not tried to scale; an unknown world became my lodestar. Mr Mulloy believed in the American dream and in education as its ladder; he just wanted Catholics on it.

Our conversations ended when I left Central, before JFK won the election on the back of Chicago corpses resurrected to vote – before the Cuban missile crisis, Sam Giancanna, Judith Exner, Frick and Frack in the White House pool when Jackie was out of town; before assassination clawed the gilt from Camelot. I made no friends at Central, rejected its ethos, returned to no reunions. But I remembered John Mulloy, who opened the borders of my mind. When I returned to Philadelphia from Cambridge and Yale, a decade later, I looked him up to thank him.

THE SEA

Sixty miles due east of Philadelphia lay another country: Barnegat Light and the sea.

Captain J. Burt

Long Beach Island is an eighteen-mile sand spit facing the Atlantic Ocean, which Barnegat Bay splits from the New Jersey Pine Barrens. The narrow island is pancake-flat except for a sand-dune spine one storey high down its entire length, a few hundred feet back from the surf; the ocean cut it in two at least three times in the last century during spring nor'easters. It has clean beaches for vacationers and the best fishing in Jersey out of Barnegat Light. Joe fished its bays, inlets and offshore waters from the time I was four and a half.

The sea is a perilous place. I went down to it for the first time in late spring 1947. My father and I, plus a nurse for him "just in case",[2] boarded a charter boat at Beach Haven to fish for flounder. A charter boat, booked in advance, fishes for whatever the "party" wants, unlike the much cheaper "head boats" that take all comers at so much a head to fish for what's advertised. We were catching flounder when the captain told us to reel in and made for a distress flare from a U-Drive garvey drifting half a mile away.

Tyros could rent small boats like garveys to run themselves – "U-Drives" – for the day. The drive-shaft came out the back end of an engine box mounted on deck amidships and down through the

2. See page 33.

deck, to form a small triangle covered by a wooden housing. Nothing covered this garvey's drive shaft: when the engine was running, the shaft and propeller-coupling rotated unprotected above the deck. One of the men aboard her had caught his trouser-cuff in the rotating coupling, shredding his leg from ankle to knee. There was blood everywhere – I saw the man's shin bone white through his flesh before my father bundled me away – and he was screaming. Our nurse bandaged his tatters, gave him a shot of morphine from a first aid kit, and we waited for the Coast Guard.

Holmes Russell ran parties on his garvey in 1947 to fish for striped bass and bluefish inshore. He was a North Carolinian from a hillbilly family, wiry, white-haired and missing three finger tips, two from his left, one from his right hand. Sun and salt water had tanned his skin almost to leather. Holmes, or "Russ" as Joe called him, grew up on the waters round Oregon Inlet, ran a still in the Carolina Blue Ridge Mountains during Prohibition and delivered white-lightning to the towns below. He could fix anything, built his own thirty-six-foot fishing boat named the *Jolly Roger*, as well as his house at Barnegat Light, and was reputed the best inshore skipper on the Jersey coast. He used the garvey to catch grass shrimp for bait and to clam in winter. The garvey was battleship-grey; on a rainy December afternoon, bent over its side jamming a pair of long-handled clamming tongs into the Barnegat mud flats, both he and it seemed wraiths.

Joe began chartering with Holmes when he still fished from the garvey. Striped bass are a prized inshore game fish: wily, hard-fighting and weighing up to eighty pounds, their white, dry flesh especially good eating. Holmes knew more about them and how to catch them than anyone else. They wintered in brackish creeks that feed Barnegat Bay, and in the spring schools of three- to five-pounders, "schoolies", headed down the Bay and out the Inlet to feed on sand-eels offshore and migrate north. Bigger fish haunted the jetties and bars of the Barnegat Inlet from spring through late fall; if you wanted big bass it was the Inlet you fished to catch them.

The shoals which stud the east coast's inlets south of Cape Cod make them treacherous gauntlets in an onshore wind; Barnegat Inlet is one of the worst. A tiara of sand-bars rings it from north to south, and sand-bar pendants choke its approaches. Dutch settlers named it *Barendegat*, "inlet of the breakers", in 1614, for the seas that rear meerschaum-white and break over its bars in the calmest weather. The Inlet is impassable when strong easterly winds pile seas on its bars. There are always a boom and roar of waves breaking; close-up they sound like rushing trains. Lines from "The Charge of the Light Brigade" come to mind as you round the Barnegat Light House and head east towards the breaking seas:

Cannon to right of them
Cannon to left of them
Cannon in front of them
Volly'd and thunder'd

For nearly 150 years men tried to tame the Inlet. The Army Corps of Engineers built two grey granite boulder jetties in the early 1900s from the Inlet's north and south shores, like a half-mile-long rock funnel, to channel water from bay to ocean and stop the north tip of Long Beach Island from eroding. The Corps had no more success than Cnut; the bars continued to grow, shrink and shift, and the Island's sands washed away. The Corps beefed them up with more rocks every fifteen years or so, to no avail.

The US Life-Saving Service opened station #17 at the Light around 1872; the Coast Guard has a well manned station there to this day. A thirty-five-foot Coastguard lifeboat, double-ended like a great white canoe with a wheel house in its middle, always lay in the Inlet in rough weather to rescue boats in trouble. She had two powerful engines and could roll through 360 degrees, right herself and stay on station. Nevertheless, one or two boats got into trouble in the Inlet every year, and one or more men were lost. Few amateurs used the Barnegat Inlet in the 1950s.

I was six my first time in the Inlet. Joe had chartered Captain Jack Sylvester's twenty-eight-foot skiff to troll for blues offshore. The mate was Sylvester's twelve-year-old son, Barty. A storm had passed offshore a few days earlier and big swells were running. They made up into breaking seas higher than the skiff's cabin top when they fetched up on the bars. The Coastguard lifeboat rolled wildly on station at the inshore edge of the north bar. Sylvester had a drink problem and may not have been quite clear headed enough that morning to realize it was not a good day to take a twenty-eight-foot skiff through the Inlet, or perhaps he was desperate for his hire. We were a third of the way out of the Inlet and taking big seas on the bow every few minutes by the time he decided to quit, but turning back was dangerous. Barty went below and came up with lifejackets, big bulky yellow pre-war canvas vests with cork blocks sewn in pockets for flotation. Joe helped me into mine and tied it tight. The critical moment would come when Sylvester tried to go about and we would be sideways to the waves rather than with our nose into them. If a sea caught us broadside we could capsize.

Joe cut an eight-foot length of rope and tied one end round his waist and the other round my left ankle. As Sylvester prepared to put the wheel over my father looked at me and said: "Whatever happens, don't let go of the rope." He had beat me, he had yelled at me, but never had he told me to do anything the way he told me to hold on to that rope. We came about in the trough of a sea and, pitching and rolling, scuttled safely back through the Inlet. That was Joe's last trip with Sylvester, who left Barnegat and his family not long afterwards. Holmes married Sylvester's ex-wife, and Barty became his step-son and the *Jolly Roger's* mate.

The favoured ways to catch stripers, requiring the most skill and with the greatest chance of catching a large one, were to chum the jetties or cast the bars. Inch-and-a-half-long grass-shrimp with shells the colour of the sandy bottom where they lived made the Barnegat jetties a buffet for stripers. Holmes would anchor within ten feet of their rocks so that a rivulet of chum, four or five grass-shrimp sprinkled from a livebait box every few minutes, trickled down the jetty from the boat. Light lines with two shrimp impaled on little black hooks floated along with the chum. There is an art to chumming: Holmes explained it to Joe the first time they anchored on the jetty – how to bait the hook, strip the line, what the trick was – then stood beside him and started catching bass. After baiting, stripping and going fishless for an hour while Holmes caught bass after bass, Joe asked him to explain again. Holmes said, "I showed you once; watch me." Joe never asked again: he fished next to Holmes for a year and a half before he caught his first bass. Most men can remember when, where and with whom they caught theirs; I was eleven, chumming on the inside of the north jetty with Holmes.

Joe with two big striped bass, circa 1948

It was a fair fight between angler and striper on the jetties: one had tackle, skill, a boat; the other, strength, sea and rocks. Big bass head for the open sea when they're hooked. You can't stop them with light chumming tackle, and a fish much over twenty pounds runs until it tires of fighting the rod-tip and reel-drag. Joe and Holmes were chumming inside the south jetty in the garvey at high tide in early spring when Joe hooked a bass he couldn't slow, a fish more powerful than any he'd hooked before. It steamed across the jetty, bound for Ireland, and would shortly either strip the reel or cut the line on the jetty's barnacles. Joe hollered, "Russ, I can't hold him," and Holmes yelled back, "Hold on!" Net boats had caught some very large bass offshore a few days before and Holmes had visions of a light-tackle world record. He started the engine, cut the anchor line and eyed the seas washing over the jetty. He picked a big one, gunned the garvey toward the rocks, cleared them and chased that bass into the open sea with Joe in the bow, rod-tip high, reeling when the bass paused. They were nearly two miles out at sea, ninety minutes later, when Holmes gaffed the striper. Not a record, but not many pounds shy.

The *Jolly Roger* lay in the wash of six-to-eight-foot high seas breaking across the north bar one fall afternoon, her party casting with light spinning-tackle for bass. Joe hooked one too strong to turn that headed for deep water beyond the bar. The only chance to land it was to follow it through the breakers into deep water. Holmes reversed the engine and backed down across the bar. The cockpit swamped, but Holmes kept going. When Joe stood beside the sixty-pound bass for photographs that evening someone asked him why he was wet almost to his armpits.

Holmes rarely cast off more than half an hour past sunrise; if one of the party was late he didn't fish with Russ that day. Barnegat Light was a ninety-minute drive from Whitaker Avenue down a two-lane highway, so Joe often left before 4 a.m. One morning he overslept and, when he started his new

1954 Chrysler Windsor, had less than an hour before the *Jolly Roger* sailed. A state trooper fell in behind him as he accelerated east from the last circle down Route 72. Joe saw the flashing light, heard the siren and held the hammer down. The chase continued at a steady 100–115 miles an hour, as fast as that Chrysler went, for 30 miles down 72, across the causeway onto the Island and north to the dock where Holmes had the engine running and all but one mooring line untied. Joe screeched into the parking lot and the trooper roared in behind. Joe leaped from the car, ran the few feet to the boat, jumped aboard and Holmes cast off. They had a good day. Two state police cruisers and four troopers were waiting on the dock to arrest Joe when the *Jolly Roger* backed into her slip that afternoon.

Heavy black rubber bags filled with iced fluke, stripers and weakfish in spring and fall, and blues, tuna and stripers in summer, rode home with Joe from the Tuesday fishing trips. Neighbours watched his car roll up our alley and hoped he'd had a good day. They came with newspaper under their arms to ask if he had fish for them. He dumped the catch, ice, blood and melt on the cement by our back drain, hosed it down and gave away what we didn't need, often most of what lay on the ground. He washed, rinsed and left the bags to dry in the garage until the next Monday night, when he loaded the car again with rods, reels, and tackle for the pre-dawn drive to

Barnegat Light. The alley smelled of fish on Wednesday mornings and local trash cans brimmed with fish heads, tails and scales wrapped in old newspapers.

Holmes and Joe fished together for ten years. After Holmes built the *Jolly Roger,* and over-fishing had decimated bass stocks, they abandoned the jetties for offshore; for the Barnegat Ridge, twenty miles northeast, to catch blues on spinning tackle till hands were too tired to turn the reel cranks; the ocean beyond for tuna up to 100 pounds, Mako sharks weighing 150 pounds, and a white marlin or two. But the *Jolly Roger* was slow, and Holmes's forte was not bluewater work beyond the Ridge, where charts, parallel rulers, compasses and protractors were needed; he never was quite comfortable farther offshore than dead reckoning could take him. It was long before the days of GPS and Holmes's reading was a little uncertain. Joe had learned almost all that Holmes had to teach him about the sea and fishing.

Ducks and geese rose quacking and honking out of the bay's salt marshes at daybreak as the charter boats headed for the Inlet. Ribbons of them streaked the skies heading north in spring and south in fall. Clouds of gulls wheeled above the bars and beyond the breakers off the beaches and dived on fleeing bait-fish. The sun rose like a new penny from the sea's edge as we'd head offshore; helmsmen squinted into it to avoid flotsam and keep their course. It died rose red and blinded them again when they were heading home. White caps form when the wind rises above ten knots and the sea backs glow mint-green. Beyond the sixty-fathom line, ocean turns magnolia green. At sea there were no vomiting drunks, no aprons with rust-brown, dried pork blood, no customers demanding cuts from the front of the case, no cops on the take, no rats behind rice sacks, no registers, no pushcart men and boys huddled round oil-drum trash fires waiting for trade. There were no Jews remembering pogroms, no hit men, no bullies. Barnegat Light was his Blessed Isles, and Joe fell in love with the sea.

After a few years, fishing one day a week was too little; Joe began to fish Wednesdays as well and muse on the long pre-dawn drives to the dock about buying a boat and becoming a charter captain. Holmes was hardly encouraging and other chartermen told him he had too much to learn before he could handle a boat in the Inlet and fish the waters offshore, and that he was too choleric to make a skipper. He bought a twenty-five-foot single-engine MayCraft early one summer in the mid-1950s, named her *Dan Rick* after his two sons in the order of their birth, and a week later took her tuna fishing. He was forty miles off when the prevailing southwesterly built to twenty miles an hour from ten, as it will on a summer afternoon, and what had been a following sea became a head sea when he came about for home. The course back was almost dead into the wind and a five-foot sea: it was four hours going and eight coming back. He took more water over the bow than ever he did again and was soaked through when he reached the dock, shaken, aware the *Dan Rick* would not serve his purpose.

Seamen say that thirty foot and over, it's the skipper, not the boat, that counts. The MayCraft was gone within days, replaced by a thirty-foot Pacemaker with twin ninety-five horsepower Chrysler engines, carvel-planked and soft-chined. She rolled but didn't pound, and made her way featly through a head sea. It's supposedly bad luck to change your boat's name; he christened the Pacemaker *Dan Rick* and so she remained when his third and final child, a daughter, was born. His third boat and then his last were *Dan Ricks* too. Joe took friends fishing on the *Dan Rick* for a few years with me as mate and began to study for a charter captain's license to take people fishing for hire. He was known as Captain Joe when he died forty years later in 1995, the only Jewish charter captain on the Jersey coast. Some said he was as good as was Holmes in his prime, but I had been gone too long to attest to that. We buried him in his fishing clothes, *Capt. J. Burt* in blue-thread script stitched across the right breast-pocket of his short-sleeved khaki shirt, *Dan Rick* across the left.

We fetched the second *Dan Rick* from the

Pacemaker yard at Forked River on a grey, windy late summer's morning. Thirty-five minutes later we were leaving the channel opposite the Barnegat Lighthouse when Joe decided to try her in a sea and headed east toward the south jetty rather than west to our dock. A palisade of breaking seas stretched in a concave arc from jetty to jetty beyond the Inlet's mouth, like a shark's jaw. The Coastguard lifeboat rolled on the north bar; there were no boats offshore. Two boat-lengths off the rocks and halfway up the south jetty it was clear that it was too rough to leave the Inlet. Joe put the wheel over to port to come about, but nothing happened. He twirled the wheel to starboard, but she did not answer. We had lost our steering in the inshore approach to the Barnegat Inlet in a twenty-five mile an hour northeast wind. Joe grabbed the ship to shore's handset, tuned the dial to the distress channel, and I heard the first and so far only *Mayday! Mayday! Mayday!* from a vessel I was aboard. The Barnegat Light Coastguard Station answered and told us to anchor up and wait for the rescue boat; it was already underway. I went forward, untied the anchors and threw and set them both.

The Coast Guard towed us to the Station where a young coastguardsman came aboard and helped us fix the steering. The *Dan Rick* left the station at about 1 p.m.; we'd been there an hour. The wind had strengthened; rain squalls blew through from time to time, hiding the salt-marsh sedge the gusts bent almost double. Joe sat on the bridge in the wind and rain, and, when we reached the channel 100 yards or so from the Station, he turned northeast toward the Inlet rather than southwest toward our dock and berth. We rounded the Lighthouse into the Inlet's approaches and picked up speed heading seaward. I called up, "Hey, Dad, where you going?" No answer. He was hunched stiff over the wheel, right hand on the twin throttles, long-billed fishing cap pulled low over his crewcut to keep out the rain and occasional spray. Twelve-foot waves built and crashed in the channel as we slammed past the tower at the end of the south jetty.

Breaking seas in the Inlet come in sets. Captains hold their boats just short of where they break, backing down if necessary (reversing to let the seas break in front of you) and count seas waiting for a lull. When the last sea breaks, the water beyond is white with foam but flat for half the length of a soccer pitch, and a boat can cross where the waves make up before the first sea in the next set builds. The *Dan Rick* was new and fast for her day. Joe shouted from the bridge, "Hold on!" and jammed the throttles all the way forward when a last sea broke. We skittered across a white foam table-top through brown spots churned from the sandbar four or five feet below, swerved right toward the south bar to avoid a sea making up, took a small wave bow-on and burst into the whitecapped open ocean. Joe sat silent on the bridge.

We circled north outside the bars and reached the north jetty about halfway down from the tower at its seaward end. The north bar is shallower, but shorter and narrower, than the others, the seas steeper, but fewer and not so wide; more dangerous if you're caught but fewer and thinner to catch you. In a blow the professionals always went in the north side. They'd sneak up alongside the north jetty, almost to the tower, keeping as close to the rocks as possible, wait for a lull, turn their bow into the bar and head across the mouth of the Inlet. When the next sea made up they turned right, got on its back and rode it like a surfboard shorewards towards the south jetty. Timed right, they were inside the bar safe home when it broke; too fast, and they overran the sea and pitch-poled; too slow and the following sea pooped them. Once committed you cannot stop. A coastguard in a life-jacket watched through binoculars from the lifeboat as Joe began his run. He turned into the bar, opened her up, caught the next rising sea and rode its back across the shoal till it collapsed well down the south jetty.

I climbed the ladder to the bridge and sat beside him for the short run to the dock. He throttled back near the marina so our wake did not disturb the boats tied there. I had started down the ladder from the bridge to handle the bow lines when he said, without looking at me, "You know, Danny, if I hadn't done that I'd have never fished again."

Mate

The author with two bluefish in the parking lot of The Independent Yacht Basin in Barnegat Light, circa 1949

I fished with my father sporadically during the years he chartered Holmes; it would have been unfair to impose an extra rod too often on the other men who shared the party's cost, even if held by a boy. My line tangled with theirs as easily as would a man's; I jockeyed for the best place along the gunwale, had to be given room fighting a fish, and by twelve could claim a man's share when the catch was divvied. But from 1955, when my father bought the first *Dan Rick*, through the '63 season, before I broke my neck, I mated for him twice a week when school was out, barring days lost to summer school.

Few vehicles shared Route 70 East with us at 4 a.m., when we headed for Barnegat, though truckers and fishermen patronized the all-night diner at the third traffic circle, where we stopped for breakfast. Suburban sprawl and strip malls had not yet gnawed the villages, truck farms, and dairies dotting the first twenty-five miles from Pennsauken, a few miles east of Philadelphia across the Tacony-Palmyra Bridge to the start of the Jersey Pine Barrens. The Barrens didn't stop then, as they do now, at a palisade of summer cottages ten miles west of Long Beach Island, but loomed for thirty uncurving miles either side of Route 72's two concrete lanes, from the fourth traffic circle to Barnegat Bay.

No road lamps, farm lights or clearings relieved the darkness through the Barrens to the sea. Colonial settlers' crops had struggled in the sandy, acidic soil; early industries – bog-iron, logging – failed; in the twentieth century the forest reclaimed it. Stubby, inflammable pitch pines crowded the road, renewed in the frequent fires summer lightning storms ignited. Road-kill included snakes, even timber rattler, raccoons, deer, squirrels, turtles, feral cats and dogs. Burning-rubber stink, thickening the air and clinging to the car, tolled a skunk's knell.

The Pine Barrens are a primeval land, where men don't belong. They occupy a quarter of New Jersey's territory, and the absence of humans in so large an area, so close to major cities – New York and Philadelphia – combined with its impenetrability, the dialect and alleged dimness of the few *Pineys* living on its outskirts, nourished tales of ghosts and ghastly murders, in the same fashion as do Louisiana's bayous. The Barrens are a popular place for Mafiosi to dispose of problems. I hunched my shoulders and scrunched down when we started through them and peered northeast for dawn's loom.

The *Dan Rick* lay tied fore and aft, plus two spring lines amidships, at the Barnegat Light Yacht Basin, which never berthed a yacht. An acrid mix of creosote-coated pilings, salt-stained teak, dried fish blood, vegetation and discarded fish entrails rotting on mud flats charged the air around her. A few young charter and commercial skippers had mortgaged themselves at mid-century to build this working marina on Barnegat Bay's tidal fringe, two water-miles from the inlet, to free themselves from high dockage fees and low catch-prices at their mainland docks, and shorten their forty-five-minute run to and from the sea; founders and locals called this dock "The Independent".

It had two sides, south for commercial fishermen like draggers and net boats, north for charter boats. The commercial dock described an *E* on its back (ш), the charter dock a backwards *E*, its three arms parallel to the shore (∃). The best chartermen, including The Independent's founders, tied up along the charter dock's front row. Part-time charter boats and a few commercial-men under forty feet rocked in their slips along the middle and outer arms, bows to shore. *Dan Rick*, the sole amateur's boat among the thirty-five in the basin, lay five slips in from the channel-end of the outer arm, farthest from the pros.

A one-storey, flat-roofed, cinderblock building, the size of a boxing ring and painted white, squatted on the parking lot's tarmac, six steps from the front slips; one half housed a walk-in ice box, the other a tackle shop. Front slips were handiest to bait-house and tarmac for loading ice, bait, and fishing parties in the morning, and for disgorging catch and fishermen to fish bags and cars in the afternoon; tourists hungering for a day's deep-sea fishing prowled them to select their hire; founders and their boats, Louie Puskas (*Gracee*), Johnny Larsen (*Miss Barnegat Light*), Charlie Eberle (*Doris May*) sailed from them for the rest of their lives, as do their grandsons sixty years later. A half-hour before sun-up we pulled into the parking lot and joined them.

Skippers – pro and tyro – turned cheeks from side to side to feel the wind, sniffed for rain, and tapped the bait-house barometer for any augury of afternoon thunderstorms as soon as they stood dockside in the dawn. Weather forecasts were subjunctive in the Fifties, before satellites, high-resolution infra-red cameras, computers and GPS combined to foretell the hourly weather precisely, days in advance, for a few square-mile patch. Nowadays, fast, twenty-four-foot fibreglass open outboard skiffs safely chase tuna a hundred miles off; in 1955 they dared not leave the inlet.

Skippers stood by the boats in clumps of twos and threes waiting for parties, or in the tackle-shop replacing gear lost the day before, and swapped information about how they'd done, where they might try that day. They were taciturn men, fourth and fifth generation Americans with Scotch-Irish (*Russell, Montgomery*), Polish (*Puskas, Kubell*), and German (*Eberle*) surnames; light skinned, excepting arms and faces leathered by sun, sea and wind; flat-bellied, ectomorphic bodies kept lean by physical labor and rolling, small-boat decks. They spoke quietly, with a slight bluegrass Carolinian drawl, curses limited to "damn" and "shit"; shouting was reserved for warnings. Talk mattered little. The catch thrown on the dock for sluicing measured captains at the end of every day. Salesmanship, clever arguments, threats and fits were equally irrelevant: if you were "skunked" – returned fishless – you had failed. You could not cheat the fish or con the sea.

They were Christians, not a Jew among them. Whatever persecution, famine or dream may have driven their forebears west was too far back for recall. Their ambition for their sons was to fish home waters; for their daughters, to marry and have kids. Doctors and lawyers did not impress them. None had a passport, nor wanted one. They were not cupiditous, and wealth did not awe them. They had a reserved contempt for "yatchies" and weekend boatmen. Barnegat Light, the Inlet and the sea were Philadelphia, Central and Pennsauken's contrapositives; The Independent's skippers my father's antitype. I wanted their world to be mine, and to be one of them.

The *Jolly Roger* lay on the first row, directly in front of the bait-house, befitting its skipper's reputation. The only fault I ever heard my caustic, cynical father find with Holmes was that blue-water sorties, beyond the Ridge's outer edge, were not his long suit. Holmes Russell was my first skipper.

I was "Danny", or "Danny Boy", to him when I first fished aboard the *Jolly Roger*, mostly "Danny" after I was nine; it was just "Boy" if I'd done something wrong, or dangerous. He taught me the rudiments of deep-sea fishing and some refinements: how to tie fishing knots in thread-line and monofilament; how to twist leader wire in a double helix so the twists lock, to bring the gaff up under a fish to impale it; how to jig for weakfish, cast for stripers, chum blues, troll tuna. I remember those lessons. But neither my fishing skills nor the rush of fighting sport fish was his enduring legacy.

"Danny, always keep one hand for the boat.

Remember, one hand for the boat" were the first two sentences Holmes spoke to me, the first time he helped me board the *Jolly Roger.* Then he illustrated what he meant by ostentatiously grasping the gunwale as he walked forward toward the cabin. I was seven then, and I reflexively grip a fixed part of any boat I board, sixty-three years later; "Keep one hand for the boat" are my first words to novices who sail with me.

From the time Holmes jumped down onto the *Jolly Roger's* deck in the pre-dawn dark, till he left her fast in the late afternoon, he watched: where and how we stowed gear, ice, bait, and food for the trip; the rods and rigs we'd use; where seas made up, and how many were in a set, as we headed out the inlet past the south jetty's rocks. He checked engine temperature, oil pressure, tachometer gauges and compass headings while making for the Ridge; observed birds working nearby and circling far off; gauged our swing if we anchored, our speed when drifting, and which way the chum streamed after he ladled it into the sea; scanned the chum slick for stalking shark fins; weighed the wind making-up after noon. Rolling home, he glanced down from time to time at the mate cleaning the catch in the stern and the dozing fishermen behind him; nothing at sea was alien to Holmes, nothing ignored. When we were about to cross one of the inlet's sand bars, Holmes always turned from where he sat at the wheel on the flying bridge and scanned the cockpit for loose gear, bait or a careless angler a big sea might toss from the boat. In good weather he warned us to hold on; in rough to move from cockpit to the wheelhouse below the bridge.

I was eleven the day I caught my first bass. We'd been shrimping the outside of the south jetty on the flood-tide for several hours, without success, and were crossing the inlet to try the inside of the north, half a mile away, as the tide began to turn. Six-foot seas were breaking on the bar we had to run to get there, and the *Jolly Roger* was not a fast boat; we would take one or more. My father sat beside Holmes on the bridge, I sat on a chair in the cockpit. Holmes looked back and down, and said, "Danny, get up in the wheelhouse and hold on," as he turned the bow northwest to face the bar 300 feet away, and increased speed. A few minutes later we reached the bar's southern edge, breasted a small wave, lifted, slammed down, and kept going. We drove through one more, slightly larger, ran another boat length, then suddenly Holmes throttled all the way back. A wave to starboard as high as the cabin-top blew the bow skyward and tossed us violently onto our port side until the gunwale lay even with the water. The Coke cooler flew off the bridge and crashed ten feet down onto the cockpit's stern. It would have killed a man, had one been in the cockpit.

I was staring out the wheelhouse window at the oncoming seas, frightened by their size, hiss and rumble as they began to break, when the cooler hit the stern behind me. The report, the sound of deck splintering, startled me; fear turned to terror. I started aft, grabbed the rail of the ladder to the bridge, and looked up to see Holmes glancing at the stern, checking for damage. He noticed me and read my eyes: "It's O.K., Danny," was all he said, in his slow cadence, his normal pitch, then turned back to the oncoming waves. The engine revved, we pounded through one more small sea, and we were across, curving west to anchor halfway down the north jetty. A decade later, when I first read Shakespeare describe a king dispelling fear, I saw Holmes looking down from the bridge:

> *. . . there is no note*
> *How dread an army hath enrounded him;*
> *Nor doth he dedicate one jot of colour*
> *Unto the weary and all-watchèd night;*
> *But freshly looks . . .*
> *That every wretch, pining and pale before,*
> *Beholding him, plucks comfort from his looks . . .*

Half an hour after we anchored up, I was seasick for the first and last time in my life, panic's after-effect as much as the seas rolling under us while we chummed. When I straightened from spewing over the leeward rail, Holmes told me to drink some Coke to dispel the tinny taste of vomit and settle my stomach. Then I tried to follow his instructions on how to strip six-pound test monofilament line from my reel, so the grass-shrimp impaled on my hook looked natural drifting towards the rocks. Shortly after noon I hooked and landed my bass.

For my father the Atlantic was an opponent, never finally floored: he contended with it every day he sailed. For Holmes, it was a homeland; there he lived, fishing, kinned with waves, sky and the *Jolly Roger*'s planking.

The sunrise drill when we reached the dock changed when my father bought the *Dan Rick*, and I became his mate. At dawn a mate readies his boat. First, he opens the engine hatches to air the bilges; in the 1950s boats under forty feet had gas engines, not the high-powered diesels of today, and every skipper had seen or heard of a boat blowing up and burning when a starter spark exploded gasoline fumes in its bilges. Next, he stows lunches, strips covers from deck and flying bridge, hauls cushions from cabins for folding chairs if the party is going blue-fishing, or wrestles fighting-chairs from dock to deck-sockets if the quarry is tuna; lifts rods from cabin-top racks and lays them forward on deck below the gunwales, to be placed in rod-holders after clearing the slip; and sets out hooks, leaders, lures, feathers. Last, he collects and stows ice, chum, bait; settles the party, and casts off.

When the car stopped on The Independent's tarmac before daylight I scooped sweaters, jackets, and lunch from the back seat and walked to the *Dan Rick,* where sea-boots, fishing-knife and scabbard, pliers and holder, and foul weather gear lived. Aboard, I went through my checklist, and, last, lifted the engine's ignition switches so Joe could fire them up. The party wedged themselves in chairs, or on a bunk below, for the two-and-a-half-hour haul to the Ridge; I cast off, and we headed east-southeast towards the inlet and the sea.

On a typical blue-fishing trip I sloshed sea water onto the chum defrosting under the starboard gunwale, to help it soften as we ran; tied nine-inch-long wire leaders – black barrel-swivel on one end, six-foot O'Shaughessy stainless-steel hook on the other – to thirty pound test monofilament on the boat rods; then turned to cutting the butterfish we'd use for bait. I unhooked the fish box where it sat against the stern, dragged it to the center of the cockpit, and swung it parallel to the keel, leaving stern and both gunwales free for fishing. Old boning-knife in hand, honed almost to stiletto, and legs spread to roll with the seas, I braced myself against the side of the fish-box, used its lid for cutting board, and began slicing half-frozen blue-tourmaline-coloured butterfish into chunks – three or four per fish depending on size. Heads and tails went onto the chum cans to sweeten their gruel, the rest into the bait-bucket in the fish-box, wedged against a block of ice to keep the chunks from softening. The boat's pitching and rolling heightened the chance of slicing off a fingertip – Holmes was missing two from his left hand and one from the right – and butcher shop training was no bad thing.

I would climb the ladder to the bridge about ninety minutes into the trip, tell my father all was ready, and take the wheel. He'd go below to check the preparations, kibbutz with the party, rest, eat the chicken his wife had prepared for him, and talk on the ship-to-shore radio to the other skippers about where they were headed, and, if any were already fishing, how they were doing. We would "go to fishing" between 7.30 and 8 a.m., depending on how long it took to find a spot.

For the next five hours I baited hooks, untangled lines, gaffed or swung fish aboard, and unhooked them; cut more bait; brought the anglers Cokes, beer, and lunch from the cooler; flushed the deck with buckets of seawater before chum and fish blood could dry; tied on new hooks and leaders when fish broke off. I said almost nothing, after the fashion of my models, the charter captains and their mates. Those were the days before factory-ships followed pelagic species like bluefish and tuna to and from their summer feeding grounds; before species like striped bass were netted almost to extinction; before countries increased their offshore national boundaries, enforced catch-limits against foreign and domestic fleets, and regulated local fishermen's catches. Today a charter boat is limited to ten bluefish per boat, and "catch-and-release" is the rule. But when I was a mate the Ridge teemed with them July through mid-October, ten fish per man was a small catch, and twenty to thirty was not uncommon if the party was competent. I often threw between 700 and 1000 pounds of gutted bluefish onto the dock when we returned, and fishermen, asked by onlookers how they had done that day, would answer, "We slaughtered 'em."

When the action heated up there was no time to gaff fish. Reach down over the side of the boat; guide the line and thrashing fifteen-pound bluefish toward you with thumb and forefinger; with your free hand grasp the wire leader below the swivel, just above the fish's jaws, and swing it aboard. Thrust the fingers of one hand under and into the gills, spread them to force the mouth open, and, with the other, work the hook loose, lift the fish by the gills, and dump it into the fish-box.

Bluefish jaws can crack walnuts, their teeth glass-shard sharp, like small man-eating sharks; they could and did sever digits from the unwary. Gloves made it difficult to feel the swivel and grasp the leader at the right spot. Gloved hands were clumsy trying to work a hook loose, especially if a fish had swallowed the bait when it struck and was hooked deep in its cartilaginous throat. The best mates worked bare-handed. The leader-wire sliced palms and fingers, gill-spines pierced finger tips. Sea water cauterized and annealed the cuts. Hands burned at day's end, heading home.

We reeled in and headed for the beach when the fish-box was full, or overflowing, or the last of the chum ladled over the side. I leaned out and down over the gunwale as we ran, to skim buckets of water for swilling deck and rods. Dip the bucket too deep and the sudden weight as it filled, added to the boat's forward momentum, could jerk your arm from its socket. The trick was to swing the bucket down to skim the surface of the waves as the boat sliced through them, so the momentum of your swing carried the bucket clear of the water as it filled. I sluiced deck and rods, stored them forward in the wheelhouse for freshwater-washing when we tied up, and set to cleaning the catch.

Bluefish rot quickly and must be gutted as soon as possible. Shirtless, feet wide apart, boning knife again in hand, I grasped the top fish in the box by the tail, lifted it clear, and laid it on the upturned fish-box lid. I stuck the knife an inch or two into the fish's anus, slit it belly to throat, grasped the entrails in the abdominal cavity with my other hand, severed them from gorge and rectum, and tossed the gutted fish on the deck astern. The entrails I threw to the terns and seagulls loitering for an effortless dinner just above the waves, a boat's length behind in our wake. In time it took less than a minute to gut a fish; within an hour or so I'd done them all, depending on catch-size, rinsed them with seawater, tossed them back in the fish-box, closed its lid, swabbed box and deck, and squared away the wheel house. There was generally a sixty-to-ninety-minute run left to the dock.

My father kept tabs on my progress from the bridge. "Danny, ya' done?" I nodded. "Geh me a Coke and come up here." I climbed the ladder to the bridge, handed him the Coke, and swung into the starboard seat. We rolled on through the sou'westerly chop. He finished the Coke and, without looking at me, said, "Here, take 'er home." I stood up, leaned forward against the bridge coaming, and grasped the wheel while he edged across behind me and started down the ladder to the deck. There was nothing said. Then he'd pause and clutch my right shoulder firmly for a moment, before lowering his torso from the bridge, and, like the *Dan Rick,* the decks were cleared. Staring west into the sun at the waves on the port-quarter, course home 300 to 305 degrees – furies, cursings, beatings and butcher shop vanished like blood and bluefish entrails through the scuppers earlier that day.

Barnegat Light

GIRLS

In the beginning, they were just cunts. A boy's role was to lay a girl as soon as he could, and then as many as possible; a girl's role, to snare the potential best provider. Sex was the coin she paid for security – something endured. The butchers I worked with, the neighborhood boys, asked, "What'd ya get" when you came back from a date, not "What was she like?" or "Did you have fun?"

A woman's place in 1958 was in the home – baking cookies, making dinner, having babies and standing by her man. My parents' marriage typified the barter basis, and 1950s middle-class American cultural organs – television, *Life*, *Look*, *The Reader's Digest* – reinforced it. The Pill was two years off, Simone de Beauvoir just a name, Germaine Greer in high school.

I learned about sex when puberty kicked in, around twelve – from *Esquire*, from forbidden *Playboys*, from the embellished exploits of older boys, from pornographic pictures slipped from hand to hand in a far corner of the schoolyard. In eighth grade our coed classes split twice a week into boys' and girls' sections for forty-five-minute Personal Hygiene classes, dubbed Sex Ed, where red-faced gym teachers explained clinical photos of mature male and female sex organs and their workings. Sex went unmentioned in mixed company; and love-making, as opposed to "Wham, bam, thank you Mam", was a pastime neither parents, family nor the men I worked with ever spoke of.

Pennsauken completed my sex education. Butchering coarsens a man; the enveloping blood, cold, steel, cutting, chopping and rotting strips life of its grace. Everything is raw, crude, brutal: pale-orange blood-flecked marrow, splintered pork loins, tubs of calves' livers marinating in bloody swill, sweating salt-back and kielbasa. My co-workers, excepting my father, were all under fifty; only one had reached his mid-forties, and they talked constantly about sex. Women were "cunt", "snatch", "poontang", "pussy", "gash", "slit", "slot", "twat", "fucks", "bangs", "tits", "boobs", "knockers", "rockers", "head lights", "pairs", "racks", "mountains", "bazooms". Their view of cunnilingus was, "Once you get past the smell, you got it licked"; of rape, "A woman can run faster with her skirt up than a man with his pants down." My father was coarsest of the lot. I spent more time with these men than with high school classmates; their view of the female became mine.

A boy had few opportunities before the sexual revolution and the women's movement to mix with girls in daily circumstances, especially if he attended a single-sex secondary school. Nice girls stayed home on school nights, Sundays through Thursdays. A teenage date, butcher-boy style, was no place to learn what girls were like. Dates were highly stylized, a Kabuki play whose purpose was sexual satisfaction: malted, pizza, or hamburger; protestation of passion; then movies, car, or other dark place to "French-kiss", "cop a feel", and, one prayed, more. Central boys could develop more rounded views of girls at "mixers" with Central's sister school, Girls' High; at parties, dances, football games, or at social events at the local synagogue. "Mixers" happened after school on Fridays; parties and dances on Friday nights; football games on Saturday afternoons; and synagogue events on Sunday afternoons: times when I couldn't attend.

I worked Fridays after school until the Mart

closed at 11 p.m. It was generally past midnight when we locked up, and the butchers made for the bowling alley across from the south end of The Mart for a beer. Sometimes I went with them, hoisted myself onto a bar stool and, short legs swinging two feet from the floor, gulped the beer they cajoled the bartender to serve a minor eight years underage. I was rarely in bed before 1.15 a.m. on Saturday mornings, woke five to six hours later to ride to work with my father at 7.30 a.m., and left work between 5 and 6 p.m. Every other Sunday, often two out of three, was a work day. I never learned to do more than shuffle through a slow dance, and – with one exception – I was twenty-two before I spent an evening *à deux* with a young woman where sex was not the aim.

Jill Rubinson stood in a corner of the den, slightly to the left of the fireplace, before a wall of books in her parents' split-level, suburban house, on a third of an acre of grass, in a costly, post-war subdivision in Lower Merion. As you turned onto the tract's entrance road, on the right hand verge, a sign atop a seven-foot-high steel pole warned, "No Commercial Vehicles Allowed". Her living room could have swallowed three of mine; as you entered, it was anchored on the left by a second ceramic fireplace, on the right by a grand piano; opposite the front door, another wall of books. The levels were un-split in the homes I knew, the walls book-less, no hearths, no dens. Their lawns were small green chin-whiskers, two bricks' length narrower than the houses they bearded, no deeper than the setback from the pavement, normally fifteen feet. Back yards, if any, were paved. I had never been in a house that was too far from neighbours to hear them quarrel, and I had never seen a girl like Jill.

She had a *gamine* air: just five feet tall, thin, flat-chested, with a bump on her nose a finger tip's width below its juncture with the skull; head large for her body, high forehead and cheekbones, skin Celtic-fair; no Gisella Bündchen, then, but come-hither cute. Sapphire-blue eyes, her strongest feature, confirmed that maternal German Jewish genes had vanquished her father's inheritance from the southern Pale. Her hair, pulled back in a short, bouncy ponytail, suited the clothes below: bobby-sox, plaid wrap-skirt, cotton shirt, all in shades of purple, the skirt's sides clamped shut just below the left thigh with a six-inch, decorative, brass-plated safety pin. Her taut body fit the cheerleader she was. But her airs, clothes, cheerleading, and no doubt padded bra were protective teenage coloration; she was her superior public high school's best student, soon to be class valedictorian, who would graduate Phi Beta Kappa from Cornell and take her Ph.D. in English Literature from Harvard. Though the den was filled with noisy teenagers flirting, "twisting", shouting in clumps and couples, she stood alone, inviolable, above us all, as if on an altar, a cleared space around her in the gaggle; a Jewish virgin princess, sceptered by right.

Academic ineptitude threw us together, mine not hers. I had begun palling around with boys from Overbrook High, met in summer school during my second remedial summer. Their neighbourhood was Overbrook Park, a small, lower-middle-class Jewish community of post-war row homes a ten-minute walk from Jill's house across City Line Avenue, in effect the other side of the tracks. Her fifteen-year-old suburban girlfriends were experimenting with social and academic inferiors and persuaded Jill to host a rare Saturday night party for them. I joined the five Overbrook boys who turned up; none of us knew Jill or had been to her house.

Ezio Pinza, an operatic bass of the period, was singing "Some Enchanted Evening", a popular song from *South Pacific*, on a forty-five record player when I walked the three steps down to the den. I misheard its first lines, "Some enchanted evening / You may see a stranger . . ." as "One enchanted evening / You will meet a stranger," thought this was that evening, and have misremembered those lines ever since. I stared across the room, met her eyes, and was felled, *bouleversé*, Michael Corleone's first sighting of Apollonia across a Sicilian field. Jill was somewhat less affected.

We dated for three months before she tired of me: six or seven times for two or three hours on

Saturday nights between March and May 1959; plus two Sunday afternoons, on one of which she was house-bound nursing a cold; and, penultimately, my junior prom. I would have called her every night and talked till the conversion of the Jews, spent every Saturday night with her, and Sundays when I wasn't working, had the choice been mine. But it was not. Her father forbade her to date me more than once every other week, or speak to me by phone more than once every other night for more than ten to fifteen minutes. There was not world enough and time.

Our dates were simple: pizzas and Cokes at Alfredo's on City Line Avenue, three blocks from her house (and the only romantic place I knew); the occasional corned beef sandwich and soda at Murray's, a mile north on City Line Avenue, with sometimes a movie first. Booths for couples lined Alfredo's walls. Tables for four and six stood in the middle of the room. White and red checkered tablecloths were set with white cloth napkins and empty Chianti bottles with candles in them, their necks thickened with dribbled white candle wax. We always sat in a booth, cocooned from other diners, Jill facing the door. Each booth had a jukebox terminal, on which I selected the *Warsaw Concerto* and Tchaikovsky's *First Piano Concerto* or *Swan Lake*, the only classical pieces I could identify. I never chose pop or country, genres I knew well. Food, music, movies, all were excuses to stare into her blue eyes and talk.

We had little in common: no mutual friends, different schools – hers wealthy, WASP, suburban, coed; mine mostly Jewish, urban, *magnet*, single-sex. Her forebears had settled – and then left – the same South Philadelphia cobbled streets as my father's people, but a generation earlier. She heard no Yiddish at home, played piano, frequented the Philadelphia Academy of Music, the museums, the main branch of the Philadelphia Free Library. Summers were spent at overnight camp in the Poconos. She had travelled, read the right books, and knew she would attend an Ivy League college as her parents had done.

Chopping blocks, hind quarters, steels, grinders, cleavers, freezer rats; drag racing, pool rooms, gang fights, suspensions, truancy; docks, jetties, feathers, chum, gaffs, seas over the bow – and sex – were alien to her. She was curious about all but the last, and I talked about them all, honoring the exception. One Sunday, desperate to see her, I drove to her house in my father's meat truck, stared at the sign at the subdivision's entrance – "No Commercial Vehicles Allowed" – and parked, like a thief, two blocks away, walking the rest of the way to her front door. She insisted on going for a ride in the truck, but I remember that sign telling me I did not belong there.

Harold and Louise, Jill's parents, had graduated from the University of Pennsylvania, one of America's eight Ivy League universities. Harold held an MBA from Penn's Wharton Business School, esteemed Harvard's equal. He and his brother inherited a large department store from their father, in the Amish country of southwestern Pennsylvania, an hour from Jill's house. Louise painted porcelain and was always flawlessly dressed, often in fine wool suits no mother I knew wore. They had a maid Mondays through Fridays, who cooked and served dinner.

Mr Rubinson answered the door when I called for Jill. He never said hello, simply called out "Your date's here." He never said goodbye. To Mr Rubinson, I was nameless. I was not offered water or soda, invited to lunch or dinner, or asked about my family or myself. On our last date but one, my junior prom, Jill descended from her bedroom in a billowing lavender dress, perfumed, her hair piled high and tight on her head *à la* Audrey Hepburn; her parents took no pictures.

Jill Rubinson, high school yearbook picture, 1961

Mr Rubinson's silent parental disdain was new to me: not a physical threat such as a punch or knife could counter. I was properly dressed, on best behavior, worshipped his daughter, and drove my father's white, late model Oldsmobile to fetch her. But none of that mattered. My offense was who I was, who my parents were, where I lived, how my father made his living, how little we had. Years before, on a fishing trip with my father to North Carolina, near midnight on a classic dark and stormy night, I wandered down the deck of the Kiptopeke Beach ferry transporting us across the mouth of Chesapeake Bay to Virginia's eastern shore, looking for a men's room. I saw a black Man symbol on a door and reached to pull it open when a hand the size of a pancake skillet materialized out of the downpour and clamped my right shoulder. The white six-footer to which it was attached drawled, "Y'all can't go in there, Boy." "Why?" "Cuz das fuh niggahs." I looked at him, bewildered; ten, I knew the word, as I did kike, sheeny, dago, mick, goy, shiksa. But what did a man's race have to do with where he could piss? Seven years later I understood; to Mr Rubinson I was a nigger.

He had nothing to fear; I had no thought of soiling his daughter. Always presentable, billingsgate in abeyance, I never laid fingers on more than her forearm, except once on the small of her back during the slow dance I shuffled through in her den the night we met. We did not "park" to "make out"; I never fumbled with her clothes. Our tongues did not touch the few times we kissed. We stopped only once at a lover's lane, that prom night, where Jill fell asleep in the crook of my white-sport-coated right arm, while Ken Klee and Mary, the couple with whom we had "doubled", petted furiously in the back. I gazed down at her for almost an hour, entranced, till it was time to drive her home. There was no need of a sword between us to keep her chaste. Jill was not a person, but a myth I dreamed to life.

I failed no more courses after my sojourn *chez* Jill, and understood that her father would not be the last adult to greet me silently if I did not go to college. But courtly love and shame would not have driven me as they did, unconjoined to indignation. Half a century on, the rage that indignation loosed stays with me.

FOOL ME ONCE

Any boy might have felt a moment's envy on the way home from his Friday night's work, passing boys he knew coming from dances and parties. But mine dissipated quickly, until I was seventeen. Others might have remarked their family's late model, expensive car, father's twin-screw sport fishing boat, mother and siblings' month-long August seashore holidays

– and might have questioned the tales of hard times and illness told to justify their working hours. Until the summer before my seventeenth birthday, I did not.

My parents' second son, Ricky, two years my junior, approached fifteen never having held a job. He was hale and several inches taller than me. My father gave him a weekly allowance for car fare, school lunches, books, movies, treats and pocket money; my mother supplemented it as needed. Now Joe said it was time for Ricky to work. Louise objected, but I thought necessity and my father would prevail. My brother joined me in the back room and on the counter in the summer of 1959.

Louise dropped him off at the Mart one late June Saturday morning. He put on butcher's coat and apron and was set to washing platters. He washed them so slowly the butchers stopped him and did it themselves. On the counter he stared past approaching customers or shuffled to serve them. Even sweeping the floor seemed beyond him. Handed a broom and shown where to sweep, he meandered across the floor, shifting sawdust and scraps from place to place to no effect. I watched the sawdust flakes spiral behind him and settle back where they had been.

And nothing happened: no beating, no punishment. His mother fetched him home at 10 a.m., two hours into his second, and last, Saturday's labor as a butcher. His allowance continued; he drove the car, never the truck. He went from Central to Gettysburg College, a respected, expensive, residential liberal arts school in southwestern Pennsylvania. Its tuition was three times that of my Philadelphia commuter college, and Joe had warned him not to apply. He enrolled there in the autumn of 1962, after Louise, unbeknownst to her husband, wrote the cheque for his first year's tuition, fees and board.

My brother's ability to refuse without consequence even to sweep a floor was an epiphany. Nine months earlier, sixteen and issued a driving license, it seemed axiomatic I would use my savings to buy a car. But title could not pass to a minor; a parent had to sign, and my father refused. Appeal to my mother would have been futile; by then warfare between us was open, mean, and continuous. After the epiphany of the broom, I toughened up.

My father was driving a year-old, white, two-door, '98 Oldsmobile that summer. Its 400-horsepower engine, four-barrel carburettor and gearing made it a blur accelerating from 0 to 60 mph. I was allowed to drive it on Saturday nights. Si Hannan, a local tough who hung out at the R&W, drove his father's 1957 gunmetal-grey Olds Super Rocket '88 – lighter than ours, with "trips", three two-barrel carburettors, on the manifold. Si's car, at least on paper, was faster.

I pulled up at the R&W around 12.30 a.m. one Sunday morning after a date. Si and others began arguing whose car was faster, and within moments his friends had put up $100, equal to $800 today. I matched it, and we headed for the dead-end at the bottom of Whittaker Avenue to find out who was right.

During the day Whittaker Avenue was a residential street, six blocks long, four lanes wide from dead-end beginning to its intersection with Roosevelt Boulevard; after midnight it was a drag strip, my house a block from the finish line. We lined up side by side near the dead end, put a friend as observer in the front seat of our competitor's car, Irv Cossrow in Si's, Harvey Webb in mine; then the juvenile shadow standing between the loom of our headlights raised his hand. We "stood our cars up", revved the motors with them in gear while applying maximum pressure on the power brakes, which lifted their rears, and watched for the shadow hand to drop. The key to drag racing is to "get off the line" at maximum speed without "burning" too much rubber; a slower car can beat a faster, if the faster spins its rear wheels for seconds because its driver applies too much power leaving the line; cooler drivers win, even in slower cars.

Eight-hundred horsepower of revving engines carries a long way on a city street in the middle of the night. My father, home from Pennsauken a half-hour earlier, left his cornflakes and went outside to see the racers pass. I got off the line with a perfect chirp of tires; the other driver spun his wheels. I was two car-lengths ahead by the first hundred feet, pedal to the metal, headed for the finish at the cross street a half block past my house. We roared past my father at over ninety miles an hour, front bumpers almost in line, but even 800 screaming horses and five rocketing tons of high grade steel and chrome could not drown his curses as we passed; he had recognized his car.

There was no sense going home. The observers settled bets, switched cars, and I took off with Irv to roam Northeast Philadelphia streets and West Jersey highways until dawn, when I would have to go home to shower and change for work at 8 a.m. I walked through our front door six hours later. Joe was hunched over his breakfast cereal. "Danny!!" I walked toward the breakfast room and stopped just shy of a swing's length from the patriarch in his chair at the head of the table, and stood, and waited. Without looking up he asked, "D'yuh win?" "Yeah." Five heart-beats, then, "If I catch you racing my car again, I'll beat you to death." We both knew I would race his car until I had my own, and that beating me to death might be more of a chore at seventeen than it had been when I was five. He had lost all moral authority the morning he allowed my brother to funk work.

On 1 October 1959, my seventeenth birthday, Joe signed for a red 1959 MGA 1600 Roadster, my first car. I wanted a hot rod, but he thought mixing a rod's speed with my temperament too dangerous. When Albert's eldest, Anita, had dropped by a month earlier in her husband's MG, my father had asked to drive it. He disappeared up the Boulevard and returned ten minutes later, confident it was tame enough, to say I could buy one. An MG wasn't what I wanted, but any car meant freedom.

My father paid me a third of a man's wage when I went to work for him; then, after a few years, half. I complained about not receiving equal pay for equal work. Mobile now, complaints ceased. "Pay me what you pay the other men, or I'll get another job." He raised my pay.

College was no certainty when the time came to apply in my high school senior year. My grades, with two exceptions, were average or worse; only one teacher would recommend me. But a butcher's nasty, brutish, short working life; the increasingly uncertain prospects in the meat business, and the contumely of my betters scotched all thoughts of butchering. I fantasized about becoming a charter captain, but that remained a romantic velleity. The chartermen's days were numbered, swamped by ninety-foot, multi-million-dollar gas-turbine head boats, carrying seventy-five fishermen a trip at so much per head. The sea would remain a mistress, not a wife.

College applications required Scholastic Aptitude Test (SAT) scores as well as high school grades. I took the SAT on Saturday, 10 October 1959, and fared better than expected, one score so high it seemed anomalous. But a high test score was a feather in the balance against twelve years dismal grades and bad behavior. My choices were few. A residential college was too expensive. Temple University, though local, cheap, and likely to accept me, was vast, with maybe 20,000 students, undistinguished, and filled with Central's strivers' lesser kin.

Mr Mulloy suggested that he approach La Salle, a Christian Brothers college where he taught nights, on my behalf. It admitted me a week later. My parents objected that it was Catholic – almost all the faculty, all department heads, the administration, ninety-eight percent of the students – and its academic standing at best no better than Temple's. I ignored them. Run by an Order founded in late seventeenth-century France to educate working class boys, its day programme small and inexpensive, an unusual destination for Central grads, LaSalle College was the best I could do.

Zaida had known more about America when he fled the Russian army than I did about LaSalle when it accepted me. He'd heard glowing tales from relatives and landsmen,[3] read about New York *yekkes*[4] in the Yiddish press, and was not the first to leave his Dnieper *shtetl* for *die goldene land.* My knowledge of the Church came from books and Mr Mulloy; of Catholics, from gangs and neighborhood fights. I'd never been in a church, and my putative Catholic relatives were no more than names. No ancestor of mine had gone to college.

I met my first religious the day I visited LaSalle. The black-cassocked Brothers floating across its small, concrete campus were aliens: quiet celibates who smiled politely as they passed, cheeks occasionally roseate from drink, robes swishing a thumb's width off the ground. LaSalle sent no summer reading list with its admissions letter, no orientation tips, no dates to meet alumni. No one said expect this, do that, prepare. But I did not want to repeat my first day's home-room gaffe at Central, four years before.

From newspapers and TV, from my mother's reverential tone when she said X or Y "went to college", I had learned to couple college and high culture, which at the time meant classical music to me. My mother would hint that an aunt Femi, supposedly an opera singer, had sung at the Philadelphia Academy of Music and taught voice at The Curtis Institute, though we never met Femi, heard her

3. People from the same shtetl or locale in the Pale.

4. Snooty German Jews, who disdained their shtetl brethren.

speak or sing, had any communication from her, or were sure if she existed. Neither opera nor any other classical music was heard in our house. Jill played Chopin on the grand piano in her living room, but not for me. My car radio was locked on WIBG, Philadelphia's premier rock and roll station, and Joe Niagra, its nationally-known disc jockey.

Two months before starting LaSalle, I changed stations; WFLN, 95.7 on the FM dial, was Philadelphia's classical music station, and mine from late June, 1960. For six weeks I tuned in, bored and uncomprehending, to the unknown – sonatas, concertos, symphonies, fantasias, tone poems, plainsong, madrigals, arias – while yearning for The Platters wailing "The Great Pretender". But the dial stayed put.

On an August Saturday just before 10 a.m., I waited in the truck on Levick Street at the intersection with Frankford Avenue for the light to change, heading for Callowhill Street's packing houses to fetch hindquarters and pork loins. August in Philadelphia is like June in Dhahran; the humid inner-city air smothered me in my soiled butcher's coat. The crossroads was cacophonous and rank: trolley cars snapping and sparking on their overhead wires, trucks and cars rumbling north and south on Frankford Avenue, a newsboy's "Inquirer! Get'cha morn'in Inquirer!", a distant, wailing siren; diesel particulates spewed from a route R bus by the curb; a sidewalk hot-dog stand added the stink of frying onions and sauerkraut. Behind me in the cab greenhead flies buzzed, scratching dried blood on the dirty brown butcher's paper carpeting the floor of the truck; on the dashboard the radio played the usual unintelligible but cultured noise.

I popped the clutch as the light changed and rattled off to get ahead of the R bus's exhaust when, from the radio, three repeated piano notes stood proud of the odor and din – *da da da; da da da; da da da* – the opening triplets of Beethoven's piano sonata Opus 14, the "Moonlight" Sonata, though I didn't know it then. Something had clicked, and for the first time I understood the relationship of one note to the next in a classical piece, and could hear it. I marked every note of its dying fall, almost a lament, and began to comprehend. I did not know it was a famous piece, that it drew on an Albinoni adagio and the Commendatore's death scene in *Don Giovanni*, nor was I familiar with its familiar name. All I knew was that the Mart receded from one piano keystroke to the next, swept away on a purifying tide of notes. The next Monday I bought my first stereo system, and my first LP, with Rudolf Serkin playing the "Moonlight" Sonata on one side, the *Appassionata* on the other. That record's midnight-blue sleeve – an image of moonlit ruins – is clear in my mind's eye, fifty-two years later.

LaSalle's entering freshmen, short-haired, beardless, and polite, lined up in College Hall in early September to register. Most wore ties, coats, and wool slacks or chinos. There were no jeans, ripped or whole, no sneakers, T-shirts, shorts, armbands, hammer-and-sickle or peace-sign buttons, no logos of any kind. Cigarette smoke filled the corridor; no one smoked a pipe. It was a few years too early for the sweet/acrid smell of pot in the air, and few of the young men would have recognized it. There were no young women; LaSalle was all male. There were one or two blacks. It was 1960, but the Sixties never came to LaSalle.

Freshmen had no electives; they chose either Science or Humanities, which determined whether their courses included Maths, Chemistry, and Physics – or History, Sociology and Economics. Everyone took Biology, Freshman Composition, two years of a foreign language, and Religion (for Catholics) or Thomist Philosophy for the heathens. R.O.T.C., the American army's Reserve Officer Training Corps, was compulsory for the first two years. Twice a week we donned heavy-wool uniforms to straggle around the athletic field in imprecise formations and smash thumbs trying to work an M1 rifle's spring-bolt. Some students, paid for by Uncle Sam, would stay in R.O.T.C. for four years, graduate in 1964 as Second Lieutenants, and head off to Vietnam as forward-artillery observers, service quite likely to get them killed there.

LaSalle was a poor college, almost bankrupt in the early 1930s and again during the war. Three large buildings anchored the campus: the five-storey, grey-brick College Hall (administrative offices and classrooms); the Student Union; and the new, whitewashed, pre-cast concrete Science Building. They formed a scalene triangle, at whose incenter stood two parallel brown-brick, rectangular, barrack-like halls, two storeys high, three bus-lengths long. The one closest to the science building housed the English faculty.

Mr Cunningham, a small, balding layman in his early thirties, taught us Freshman Composition in a first-floor classroom of the English hall, from 10 a.m. till 11 a.m., Mondays, Wednesdays and Fridays. We read and discussed short stories, a novel or two, a few poems, a Shakespeare play (perhaps *Julius Caesar*), and wrote short essays as directed. Freshman Comp was an American college course devised, in part, to hone students' writing skills; even Ivy League universities required it. I had written what was demanded at Central, and got by, but no attempts at fiction or poetry or diary-keeping.

At the close of Mr Cunningham's first class he asked us to write 750 words on someone we knew and hand them in that coming Friday; his only instructions were as to length and form: in ink or typed; on standard 8.5 by 11 inches paper; folded in half lengthwise; our name, his name, and class

(English 101) in the middle of the outer sheet's right-hand fold. I wrote about Holmes Russell clamming the tidal flats of Barnegat Bay from his garvey in a grey November drizzle. My father had pointed him out to me one day in the early 1950s, when we were crossing the causeway from Long Beach Island to the mainland, and the image stuck. I imagined standing beside Holmes, in piercing salt cold, stomach muscles knotted, straining to close a clam rake. Sixty years on, I see him:

He jams his clam tongs down three feet
and fetches bottom, pulls them so wide
he leans spread-eagled, then scissors
back, heaving till his knuckles meet,
and hoists the bales over the side
hoping for little necks or oysters,
a black oil-skinned stick figure
pile-driving in November sleet.

Dennis Cunningham hurried into class through the door to our right a few seconds past ten the following Monday, plopped a bundle of folded essays on the pale oak table near the window, took a breath. He opened the top paper on the stack and began to read. He was into the second paragraph. I lowered my head. He finished, looked around the room: "Mr Burt? Here." He handed me my paper with a nod of approval, then gave the others theirs.

I had put my back into that first college week: attended all my classes, completed all assignments, read the articles for Sociology and History on reserve at the library. The Holmes essay had not come easy; it was the product of drafts and blotted lines, a process new to me. There would be no more chances if I failed. Mr Cunningham's enthusiasm convinced me what LaSalle required I could do. On that proof, rather than self-belief, I've built.

A week earlier, college had meant trade school to me, leading to a degree and white-collar job. Not any longer; nothing had satisfied me so intensely as producing those two pages. Mr Cunningham beckoned as we were leaving class, told me his office hours, and asked me to stop by. When I did, he encouraged me to write for *The Collegian*, the student newspaper, and perhaps the quarterly literary magazine. A few weeks later *The Collegian* published my first editorial.

LaSalle students with consistently high grades qualified for the Dean's List, which conferred the privilege of skipping class. I was on the List from the end of my first term, and I used the freedom to read at the direction of Bob Smith, a thirty-year-old English Literature professor at LaSalle and Ph.D. candidate at the University of Pennsylvania. We met when I took his survey course, "Chaucer through Eliot", in the fall of my sophomore year, and fell in lasting love with English poetry. He began suggesting books – poetry, fiction, criticism, history of ideas – then spent hours discussing and arguing about them with me in his office, or in an Irish bar a few blocks away. For two and a half years Bob labored to remedy my literary and cultural gaps. He played Henry Higgins, and, by my senior year, I no longer sounded like Tony Soprano when I was sober. Drunk or furious, I revert to type. Bob would have remained a friend had he not suffered severe brain damage in the car wreck in which I broke my neck. My poetry chapbook *Certain Windows* is dedicated to him.

Sophomore year I began struggling to write poetry, while continuing to contribute sporadically to *The Collegian*. LaSalle's literary journal published two of my haikus. Shortly after they appeared, a professor in the English faculty asked what I would like to do when I graduated. "Write." "Do you have anything to say?" I didn't answer, believing that I did not. For the next forty-three years I made notes and drafted poems, but kept them to myself. Six years ago I asked a typographer to design a font for a stele I was erecting on land I own, and, at his request, sent him the sonnet intended for it. After reading it, he asked, "Do you have more?" – "A few." – "May I show them to Michael Schmidt, *PN Review*'s editor? I design their covers." Had he not done so, I doubt I would have published more poetry than those two college haikus.

The reception of the Holmes essay and my college life went unmentioned to my parents. My first two-and-a-half years in college I studied and slept at home only during the shank of the week – after which I moved out completely. College life – reading, studying, writing, talking – occurred either on campus, at local bars, or at my girlfriend's house in Overbrook Park, where, from the time I entered La-Salle, I ate, read, wrote, fornicated and was made welcome.

A gaggle of shrieking teeny boppers file through the City Line Avenue bowling alley's doors and start down its steps as I swagger up them on a dateless Saturday night in January, 1960. Prominent in the rank of parked cars opposite is my shiny, now customized and hopped-up MG. One of the girls is short, thin, heavily made-up, seventeen I guess, and prettiest of the lot. Her name is Sharon Guard.

I haven't seen Sharon or her friends before, nor have my two companions from Overbrook High. Our three heads turn as one. Her short skirt leaves a long clear run for her fish-net stockings, and prominent breasts part her car coat. I stare – big black hair, pale skin, Norman nose, white teeth in bondage to braces. I try a pick-up line, she parries, and in five minutes she is sitting beside me in the passenger seat of my roadster while we joyride around her neighbourhood. Two months shy of fourteen, she'll be jail-bait for another two years, but she jumps in my car with the brio of the older girl she looks.

We date frequently in the following months; our phone calls are unlimited; she has a generous curfew; her mother is eager for us to go steady. It is not an untumultuous romance; I am certainly unbesotted. We break up every five weeks or so, I date other girls, but she remains my default squeeze. At dawn after my high school senior prom, we lie grappling on the sofa in her living room, when she says suddenly "Tell me you love me, and things will be different." Two things are certain: my glands ache for things to be different, and I do not love this fourteen-year-old girl. I don't exclaim, "I love you" and rip off her bodice; I think about what to say; wrestle with my answer. Then I lie, and things are different, not completely at a stroke, but soon enough to satisfy me.

Sharon covered her school notebooks with my name. She changed how she spelled hers to conform to how I pronounced it; for decades after we were disentangled she continued to spell Shairon, rather than Sharon as in the Bible and on her birth certificate. Her hair, teased and heaped when we'd met, now hung long and straight just above her shoulders; her make-up lightened; she frequented Lord & Taylor; she became an emblem of the Ivy League, coed look I favoured, a precursor to Ali MacGraw in *Love Story* a decade later. But unlike pre-pill coeds, she never had a headache and she quickly mastered sophisticated sex.

Dorothy "Dot" Guard promoted her daughter's desires; what Sharon wanted, Dot helped her get. A poor cook, but master of take-out, Dot ministered to my penchant for hamburgers and fries from Bassin's; corned beef, potato salad and sour tomatoes from Murray's; pizza from Alfredo's; Chinese from the Mandarin Kitchen on Sundays after work; all were available on demand. Her son, Melvin, slept in his mother's bed so that I could sleep in his room. Dot knew that her daughter and I were sexual partners; once, through the basement window, she glimpsed us double-backed but turned a blind eye.

Jack Guard, Sharon's father, sold newspapers and wrote numbers[5] from a sidewalk kiosk at Fifteenth and Market Streets in center city Philadelphia, a block from the statue of William Penn atop City Hall. The racket allowed his family to live in the lower-middle-class neighbourhood of Overbrook Park. Jack left for work before 5 a.m. each morning, and went to bed by 8 p.m. Dot had the stronger personality and dominated the family. If Jack objected to the drama playing out in his house, he never said so to me.

5. See footnote on page 13.

My father warned me more than once on our pre-dawn drives to the *Dan Rick* that an early marriage was inevitable. He crudely adduced Sampson, "One hair on a woman's cunt is more powerful than the strongest man on earth," and painted Sharon as a succubus, her mother as co-conspirator. But a quiet place to study, calm meals, feminine affection, and testosterone all shouted him down.

Sharon was sixteen and a half and five months gone when she told me she was pregnant. It was early October of my junior year, just after I turned twenty, and the leaves were red and gold, still crisp, crackling when you trod them. Pennsylvania's autumn swan-song was never so vibrant again. She had been radiant that summer, sweet sixteen, an hour-glass in a scarlet one-piece swim suit; now we knew why. Morning sickness vexed her, but she said nothing; no one noticed. We told our parents. They assumed we would marry.

I refused. After a half-hearted effort to change my mind, my father defended my decision. My mother's view had no weight. It was too late for an abortion; the baby would have to be given away. The Guards were not opposed; Dot was more fearful of local gossip should her daughter become an unwed mother. The sticking-point was Sharon.

My father's first meeting with Sharon was to

persuade her to surrender her unborn. They clashed as equals in the living room of our house. Joe's logic, persuasion, inveigling, promises of a bright, child-free future for the two of us, threats, shouting – changed nothing. She left him astonished at her fortitude and determination to keep the child. In the end, she did not give it away.

A few weeks later she began to show and moved to a home for unwed mothers ten minutes' drive from her house. The understanding was that she would offer the baby for adoption; the sop was that we would then marry – an uncertainty with the child gone. But the home had a telephone, and once a day Sharon called. She wrote every day as well. I took her calls, read the letters; their unvarying themes were loneliness, fear and betrayal; their unvarying demand, my assurance that if she gave up the baby for adoption I would marry her. Her tears provoked mine; each reassurance compromised me. One night, six weeks into her stay, trying to prepare for class, I blacked out. When I came to I called Sharon and told her I would pick her up the next day and drive south to a state where we could marry without parental consent.

Early evening the next day, in a cheap motel outside Elkton, Maryland, Sharon's water broke. An ambulance took her to the local hospital while I followed in my car. Two months premature, after long labour, she gave birth to a tiny girl. The preemie died in an incubator, unnamed, a few hours later; I had seen it, Sharon had not. I authorized its disposal, told Sharon the newborn was dead, and married her two days later, an hour after she left hospital. *Dele iniquitatem meam*.

We stitched up lives and education: Sharon returned to Overbrook High's eleventh grade, half a year behind her class, and went on the pill; I rented a cheap apartment for us in an iffy neighbourhood, apologized to professors for late papers but did not explain, worked longer hours at the Mart. Law school loomed, though I'd never met a lawyer. Neither politics nor law enthralled me; what workings I'd seen of both were venal and corrupt. Stocks, bonds, property, trusts, multinational business and finance – meaningless constructs in economics textbooks.

"Words alone are certain good" was what I knew then. In the small, still place where faith hides from reality, I still believe that. Marvell, Wordsworth, Yeats, Eliot, Auden I read, reread and remembered. Brooks, Warren, Ciardi, Blackmur guided me. I took my sense of form from Americans: Ransom, Lowell, Stevens, Sissman. But I had no academic calling; I lacked the faith in people, reason, and the human capacity to change that teachers need; academic disputes, journals, publish or perish left my pulse unquickened. The social requirements for advancement in an American university's English department would have been beyond me.

Most of all, I was afraid: of the Depression-era poverty that my father and the butcher shop drip-fed into my blood; of the penumbral Gentile world that might take every stick and loaf without reason, warning, or recourse; of the relegation my lack of pedigree foretold. Fear trumped love. It almost always does. LaSalle's English faculty pressed me to pursue a Ph.D. in English – but lawyering, the default choice for American liberal arts graduates, was mine.

There was no faculty lounge in the English hall. Two professors shared each faculty office, and there they and fellow English teachers would gather to swig soft drinks, sip tea brewed on a hotplate, argue about literature, and pass the bruit of the day. My last two years I usurped a corner in Bob Smith's office and took part in these conversations. There, a few days after the Kennedy assassination in late November, 1963, four faculty were battering me with arguments for graduate school rather than law school. A newcomer asked, "Have you thought about going to Oxford or Cambridge?"

John Eldergill, an Englishman on a year's teaching-exchange between LaSalle and a minor English public school, had been up at Downing College, Cambridge, and studied under F. R. Leavis. My world was bounded by two Philadelphia neighbourhoods and Barnegat Light; I had read of Oxford and Cambridge, but attending them was inconceivable. Eldergill asked if I had written anything that might be publishable. I thought of an essay I'd done on T. S. Eliot. He suggested I send it, with recommendations and a personal letter, to Balliol College, Oxford, and to Trinity and St John's Colleges, Cambridge. "Who do I send them to?" – "Senior Tutor, Balliol College, Oxford, and Trinity and St John's Colleges, Cambridge."

Over the next two weeks I assembled the ersatz applications, and shortly after Thanksgiving, in the last days of November, mailed them to England, one each addressed to "The Senior Tutor" at the colleges he named; no street addresses, their salutations "Dear Sir". I mentioned no wife, having left Sharon intending to divorce.

After dinner on December 26, 1963, Boxing Day in Britain, I start in my roadster with Bob Smith for the Modern Language Association Convention in Chicago, a third of a continent west, to get a better sense of what graduate work in English will mean if I decide against law school. We stop just beyond Pittsburgh for coffee, and I take another antihistamine to quell the symptoms of a cold. Snow begins to fall lightly. An hour later, shortly after midnight on the Ohio turnpike near Ravenna, I doze off at the wheel.

The lights of a sanding truck startle me awake perhaps twenty feet from its tailgate. I yank the wheel left to avoid hitting it; the car jack-knifes and slides towards the medial ditch. I spin the wheel hard to the right but can't get traction. We run off the road and begin to flip. As the rear end rises, I think, "Well, here it goes. I've had mine." The roadster flips end for end, and my head slams the ground; there is no roll-bar. I come to in the wreck, death rattling in my unconscious passenger's throat, and I cannot move, nor even wiggle my fingers.

I waver in and out of consciousness, am dragged from the wreck, and open my eyes again on a gurney in an ambulance, my teacher's rasping gurgle the only human sound. I keep asking, "Am I going to die?" until the attendant says, "No, no; why keep asking?" – "Because I don't want to make a fuss if I am."

For eight days I lay comatose in a small rural hospital in Ravenna, Ohio, waking only once, briefly. My father was by the bed. Ashamed of my paralysis, I screamed "Go away! Get out of here! Leave me alone!" He left.

They took me for x-rays when I emerged from the coma. I was paralyzed from the neck down; below my chin only my left little toe was sensate. Whiplash, they thought. Orderlies tried to lift me into a wheelchair to go to radiology; pain knocked me out. When I came to, the orderlies wrapped a towel around my neck to stop it lolling, and asked if I could bear the pain. "Yes." I was rolled off, blacking out intermittently until the x-rays were done.

I woke at dawn to a nurse and orderly packing sandbags around me under the direction of the local neurosurgeon. My neck was broken; the fifth and sixth cervical vertebrae had mashed the seventh and crushed, but not cut, the spinal cord. The surgeon told me that he planned to fuse my neck: take a bit of bone from the hip, insert it between the crushed cervical discs, and pin the lot together. "What happens if your hand slips?" I asked for a second opinion.

The doctors decided to try Crutchfield traction first, to see whether the vertebrae might heal themselves. Orderlies bolted a triangular steel armature with a pulley at its apex to the head of the bed, eighteen inches beyond and three inches above my head. One shaved my skull, and the neurosurgeon drilled two holes towards the rear of its crown. He augured in two stainless-steel eye-screws, threaded two filaments of fine stainless-steel wire, each five feet long, through each screw eye, wound them round the eyes like guy-lines around tent pegs, then twisted them tightly around each other to form a braided wire queue. Last, the surgeon draped the queue's running end over the armature's pulley, passed it through the eye of a large hook, and wrapped it round to secure it. The orderlies placed bricks under the two forward legs of the bed frame, so it sloped at a twenty-degree angle from head to foot, and suspended weights from the hook now dangling below the pulley.

Crutchfield traction is a medical rack, with gravity the Torquemada: the weight of your body drags you down the inclined bed, while the weights dangling from the pulley haul your head up towards the armature. Weights are added or subtracted from the hook until the opposing pulls balance, relieving pressure on the neck. The crushed vertebrae unclench the spinal cord, return to their proper position and heal, as broken bones do, if you're lucky. But as the tug of war between head and feet pulls rope, neck muscles and cervical vertebrae apart, their creeping, remorseless separation builds the pain, akin to what women endure in childbirth. The first forty-eight hours were the worst.

I was awake, unmedicated, silent, pinioned to this machine. The pain from separating bone and muscle began to build when they hung the weights on the wire. I called for my first shot of pain-killer, allowed every four hours, was injected with morphine, and slept. But that first evening the wings of morphine could not carry me away for long; my eyes snapped open in the darkness with two hours left before I could call for my next dose.

Pastor William McCabe, Pastor Bill, a large, gentle Lutheran minister, made a daily round of seriously ill patients. That first evening he visited me. He stood by the bed for an hour while I confessed all I was ashamed of, said how talking to him helped shunt the pain aside, how grateful I was, though an atheist then and now, to have him standing there. Finally, he said he'd promised to visit a woman dying of cancer one floor above. A few minutes later they gave me a second shot.

The pain dwindled after a few days. Worried about addiction, I weaned myself from the morphine. Pastor Bill appeared less regularly, for shorter visits. Three months later a nurse buckled me in a stainless-steel and leather strap brace from hips to chin, gently raised me from my bed to grasp a medical walker, and shuffled beside me as I began relearning how to walk. When my father came to take me back to Philadelphia I did not mention Pastor Bill.

We flew to Philadelphia and drove to my parents' house for dinner. My mother and Sharon, with whom I had reconciled while I lay knitting, had dinner waiting. At table, my father, seated to my left in his customary place at the head, asked me to pass the thick, green-glass quart bottle of Canada Dry Ginger Ale that served for our champagne. I could not lift it. He blenched: his strength could do nothing for me now.

Two hours later I laboured up the stairs in the middle of the afternoon to a furnished first-floor flat Sharon had rented in a poor section of Germantown, ten minutes by car from LaSalle. The phone rang as we entered; I hobbled over and managed to lift the receiver. My mother said, "Danny, there's a letter here from England. I don't know anybody in England." – "Who's it from?" – "J. A. Crook, Tutor." – "Open it up." She began to read:

St John's College, Cambridge
25th March 1964

Dear Mr Burt,
The College Admissions Committee instructs me to say that it has agreed to offer you a place here to read for the B.A. Degree in English, beginning in October this year. I am sorry this answer has been long in coming, and I hope it is not too late.

Yours sincerely,
J. A. Crook, Tutor

It was not too late.

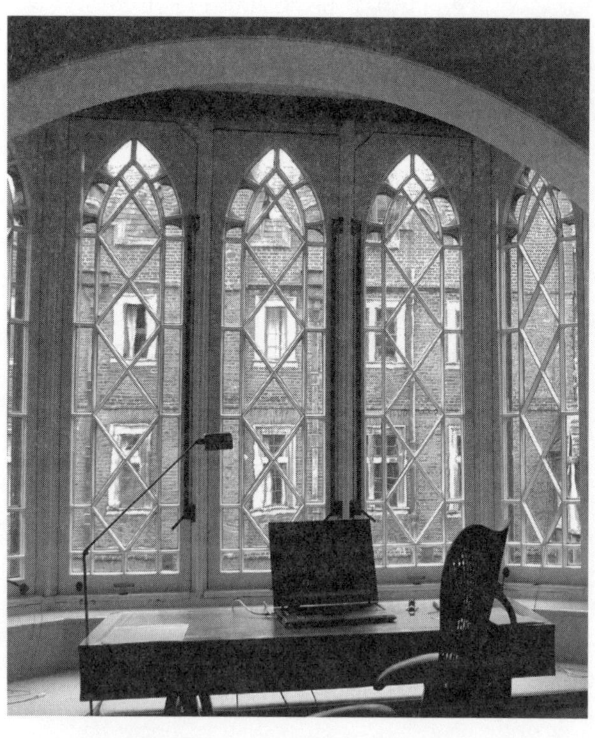

The author's set in New Court, St John's College, 2013

IV

– Envoi –

London

I live in London now, my countrymen are Britons. Thomas Wolfe maintained that you can't go home again – literally true in my case. Almost all the men and women in this story are dead. Three of its worlds are gone, the last changed utterly.

The "I" claims less attention toward life's end; a parvenu's minor failures and successes interest no one. I wrote *Certain Windows*, which appeared with my poems in a chapbook of the same name, at my publisher's urging, after he learned more about me and the stories behind some of my poems. Since I had no ready reply to those who read *Certain Windows* and asked what took me from 716 South Fourth Street to London SW7, I wrote *No Expectations* in search of answers. I found them in the places, people, and incidents set down here. A misremembered line from Yeats, words in a quatrain Auden struck from his famous elegy for Yeats, these sum it up: lust, rage, and a dream of writing well.